William James Ashley

Nine Lectures on the earlier constitutional History of Canada

William James Ashley

Nine Lectures on the earlier constitutional History of Canada

ISBN/EAN: 9783337187736

Printed in Europe, USA, Canada, Australia, Japan

Cover: Foto ©ninafisch / pixelio.de

More available books at **www.hansebooks.com**

NINE LECTURES

ON THE

EARLIER CONSTITUTIONAL HISTORY

OF

CANADA,

DELIVERED BEFORE THE UNIVERSITY OF TORONTO IN
EASTER TERM, 1889,

BY

W. J. ASHLEY, M.A.,
*Professor of Political Economy and Constitutional History in the
University of Toronto.*

Late Fellow of Lincoln College, Oxford.

TORONTO:
ROWSELL & HUTCHISON,
PRINTERS TO THE UNIVERSITY.

1889.

TO THE

STUDENTS OF THE SECOND YEAR

In the Department of Political Science in the University of Toronto.

WILL you let me dedicate these lectures to you, and ask you to accept the written in place of the spoken word ? You will observe that they barely reach down to 1791. Once I thought that I might, without any very considerable labour, arrive at conclusions to lay before you on all or most of the important questions which the history of the Dominion involves. But when I came to 1791 and looked across the gulf to 1867 ; when I read the titles of all the works already written upon the period as they are collected in Mr. Reade's recent papers in *Canadiana;* still more when I turned over Mr. Brymner's *Calendars* of unprinted historical MSS. ; may I confess that my heart sank within me ? Here was a sufficient task for one man's strength : and yet on the other side Economics were crying out with still louder voice for all the attention I could give. You will not think it strange that I should decide that for the present the social and industrial problems of Canada and America demand all my energy. Deciding thus, it occurred to me that it would be a still further saving of time on your part, and on mine, if, instead of annually redelivering for the next few years those few lectures on the Earlier Constitutional History to the preparation of which I had been able to give some little care, I might as well call in the aid of the printing press. Nobody will suppose that they claim any more authority now that they form a "book;" and I trust you will not fail to let me know if any of the statements they contain seem exaggerated or unfounded. We may hope that by-and-by Canada's greatest University will have one among its teachers who can devote his main strength to Canada's history; and that a long series of special studies, like that on the Ontarian township, which one of my pupils has already prepared, will furnish the material for a satisfactory treatment of the whole constitutional development. Meanwhile, this little pamphlet, read in conjunction with Dr. Bourinot's two admirable essays on *Federal* and *Local Government*, may perhaps help you to discover some of the broader outlines of Canadian history.

CONTENTS.

		PAGE.
Lecture	I.—On the Nature of Constitutional History	7
"	II.—On the Aristocratic Character of the Earlier Colonies	18
"	III.—On the Early Lieutenants-General	27
"	IV.—Of the Company of New France, and of the System of Government introduced in 1663	37
"	V.—On the Expulsion of the Acadians	49
"	VI.—On the Beginnings of Representative Government in Nova Scotia	62
"	VII.—On the Struggle between England and France, and the Conquest of Canada	70
"	VIII.—On the Policy of the Quebec Act	79
"	IX.—The same Subject, continued	91

THE EARLIER CONSTITUTIONAL HISTORY OF CANADA.

LECTURE I.

On the Nature of Constitutional History.

BEFORE we address ourselves to the constitutional history of Canada in particular, it may be worth while to call your attention to the ambiguities which lurk in the terms "constitution" and "constitutional history," and to make clear the sense in which the term "constitutional history" will be used in these lectures. The original meaning of "constitution" is, of course, the way in which a thing is made, the manner in which it is arranged, its putting together, its nature. With this agrees the original meaning of the German term which is used as its equivalent : *Verfassung*—a thing's composition, the character of its construction, the arrangement of its parts. In this sense we can talk of *any* state as having a constitution, and a constitutional history. Every state, by the mere fact that it is a state, *i.e.*, something more than a disconnected number of individuals who chance to live near together, must needs have some form, some characteristics, which cause it to resemble or differ from other political societies : there must be certain ways in which the various elements or parts of which it is composed affect one another. Using the word in this way, Russia or Turkey has a constitution just as much as France or Switzerland.

Early in the 18th century, or even earlier, the word came to be used in a narrower sense, as meaning not only the way in which a government was as a matter of fact carried on, but the way in which it ought to be carried on, and more specifically, certain rules or recognized principles by which the arbitrary authority of rulers was restricted. Thus Bolingbroke in his *Dissertation upon Parties*, writes, "If this [the freedom and independence of parliament] be shaken, our constitution totters. If it be quite removed, our constitution falls into ruin." In this sense, to take another example, it could be said that during the 18th century, "*Habeas Corpus* was part of the British constitution," by which was meant that it was claimed by the nation generally, and recognized by the Courts and the Executive, that if a man were detained beyond the time really necessary to arrange for a trial, without being brought to trial, his friends had a right to set a process at work which would procure his speedy delivery—or to put it shortly, freedom from arbitrary imprisonment was a recognised part of the British " constitution " at that time. There is, however, a natural tendency to antedate ideas and institutions,—a tendency especially strong in England, where almost every constitutional struggle was regarded by, at any rate, a large part of those engaged in it on one side, as an endeavor to regain or to confirm ancient liberties. Accordingly, the practice has grown up of judging events by a later standard—of calling some action of the government unconstitutional, when, as a matter of fact, the principle which it violated had not yet been generally recognized. In cases like these, the adjective more fitly to be applied would perhaps be "tyrannical," or "unjust," or perhaps not more than " unwise."

From this use of the word came the term "constitutional monarchy," as the common equivalent for limited monarchy. The circumstances of the latter part of the 18th, and of the early part of the 19th century caused this term to receive a still further limitation—to be applied to states which had a king as the possessor of executive authority, but in which there was associated with him a council or parliament, representing or supposed to represent the people at large, or such part of them as were thought worthy to have the suffrage, and having power, either alone, or in conjunction with the king, to determine the manner in which that executive authority shall be exercised. It is in this sense that the author of a well known school history, calls the period from 1485 to 1688, the period of "personal" monarchy, and that from 1688 to our own time, the period of "constitutional" monarchy.

Then, as nations rose to overthrow the old order, they began to demand not only that governments should be limited, but that the limitations should be written down; and thus came the last use of the term "constitution," for the document which determines the character of the various powers in a state, and the limits of their action. In this sense France and the United States have constitutions, and England has not; and in this sense Canada has a constitution so far as certain parts of her political life are concerned, and has not so far as others are concerned.

There are thus at least three senses of the term constitution: the way in which as a matter of fact a country is or has been governed; the way in which it is supposed a country should be governed; and an instrument setting forth a method of government: and in addition, *constitutional* has come to be used as descriptive of a particular form of limited monarchy. Which of these meanings should be had in view when we address ourselves, in this department of Political Science, to the study of *constitutional* history? That will depend upon the object we have in view. If our purpose is that of the constitutional lawyer, whose object is to anticipate or influence the decision of a court of justice on a constitutional question submitted to it, all we need study, in countries which have a written constitution, is, the text of this document, the legislative enactments by which it has been given effect, and the legal decisions by which it has been interpreted. In England, which has no written constitution, all we need study are the Acts of Parliament relating to the subject, and the legal decisions interpreting them. Great as the differences are, the frame of mind in which the constitutional lawyer approaches a question is in Canada, the States, and England, very much the same : in each he must have regard to certain documents and cannot go behind them. He has no right, as a constitutional lawyer, to introduce either political or moral considerations. Imagine, for instance, that the constitutionality **of the law** passed in some of the Southern States forbidding anyone to teach a negro to read, had been in question before a United States court : all that the lawyers would have had any right to consider would be whether the education of negroes was one of the matters reserved to the United States Congress by the "constitution"; and whether, supposing it was not, the state enactment had been passed according to the forms laid down in the Virginian "constitution." Precisely the same is true of England, save that there Acts of Parliament take the place **of** a written constitution. **If,** for instance, Parliament, meaning of course thereby **the Queen,** Lords, and Commons, and not the **Commons alone,** were to pass an Act conferring the franchise upon all persons above the age of fifteen : the Judges would refuse to listen to any argument as to the wisdom or unwisdom of such a measure : counsel could only argue that the statute did not mean what it was alleged to mean : not that, granting it to mean so and so, it was foolish or immoral.

Owing to the character of the political system of the United States, constitutional law, as I have thus defined **it, has** obtained an importance vastly greater than in any other country. With the growth of new provinces in the Canadian Dominion, and the increasing complexity of **modern** life, constitutional law will come to occupy a similar position here. And as constitutional *history* is not unlikely to fall into the hands of constitutional lawyers, there is some danger lest they should be unduly influenced by their professional habit of thought, and should take that narrow view of constitutional history which identifies it with the description in order of time of a number of constitutional instruments. Indeed, a modern Canadian writer expressly defines constitutional history in this way. He says :

"This year, 1887, is the centenary of the United States constitution, and the amendments to the original document can be comprised in less than two pages of an ordinary book. These changes and the decisions of the supreme court of that country are the basis and *substance* of the United States constitutional history. So it is and will be in this country, though the amendments are effected in a different way, and the judicial interpretations may come from any of our courts."

This, which may be called the lawyer's conception of constitutional history, however satisfactory for the lawyer's purpose is, as I would have you believe, inadequate from the point of view of political science. For our purpose is to try to understand what the real character is of the political society we are considering. Constitutional instruments may mark the stages in development may; even come, as it were, to have a strength of their own and serve as the barriers within which political life must move; but just because they are constitutional instruments and not lengthy treatises they cannot explain themselves, and they cannot determine the use that will be made of them. To use an obvious example, suppose we knew nothing whatever of the constitution of the United States except the document called the "constitution," should we be able to form any picture of the actual working of its political system ? The constitutional document says nothing whatever of the existence of *party* ; its framers expected that

the persons chosen as presidential electors would have a
real freedom of choice. We know very well that the only
two persons between whom the choice can lie, are selected
at party conventions, and that the voting of the chosen
electors is now a matter of form. In the same way we
should be unable to discover from the constitutional document that the Senate would begin with being "essentially
a diet of plenipotentiaries," * or "international conference," † and that it would become by our own time an
Upper Legislative Chamber : no one would guess that
the expectation of the founders of the constitution that
the House of Representatives would obtain a position like
that of the English House of Commons would have been
so signally defeated, and that it would sink into a position
subordinate to the Senate. ‡

To illustrate the inadequacy of the study of constitutional documents in relation to Canada, look at the sections
in the B. N. A. Act referring to the Executive:

Sec. 9. "The Executive Government and Authority of
and over Canada is hereby declared to continue and be
vested in the Queen."

Sec. 11. "**There shall be a Council to aid and advise in**
in the Government of **Canada, to be** styled the Queen's
Privy Council for Canada : **and the** Persons who are to be
Members of that Council shall be from Time to Time
chosen and snmmoned by the Governor-General, and sworn
in as Privy Councillors, and Members thereof may be
from Time to Time removed by the Governor-General."

Sec. 12. Powers under any previous Imperial or Provincial Act "vested . . . in the respective Governors or
Lieutenant-Governors, . . with the Advice, or with the
Advice and Consent, of the respective Executive Councils
thereof, or in conjunction with those Councils, or *with
any number of Members thereof*, or by those Governors
or Lieutenant-Governors individually, shall, as far as the

* Bryce, *American Commonwealth*, I., 118.   † *Ibid*. 121.   ‡ *Ibid*. 125-127.

same continue in existence and capable of being executed after the union, . . be vested in and exercised by the Governor-General **with the** Advice, or **with the** Advice and Consent of, or in conjunction with the Queen's Privy Council for Canada, or **any** Members thereof, **or** by the Governor-General individually, as the Case requires."

In reading these clauses, we, and indeed the **writers of** constitutional text books, have in our minds **some knowledge of** the Cabinet or Ministerial system; and *we explain the document in the light of that knowledge.* But who, coming to the **document** without any such previous knowledge, could guess that "any members thereof" meant a small body of men, all of the same opinions on every important political question, holding the chief executive offices, and at **the same** time possessing **the confidence and** commanding **the votes of the** members **of one of two** great political **parties; and also that that party needed to have a** majority **in the Lower House of the Dominion** Legislature? It would **be in vain that we fell back on the** assertion with which the **preamble of the Act begins, that the** Confederation is to have **"a constitution similar in** principle to that of the United Kingdom"—for **no British** Act of Parliament so much as mentions the Cabinet. **We** cannot understand, therefore, one of the most important parts of the Canadian system, **without** going behind constitutional documents to the general **political and** social history of the people.

When we do go **back to the** history of a state, we find that it is a history in **the main** of slow and general **development.** It is **in** History **as it is in** Geology: thirty or forty **years ago geological changes were** explained **as the** results **of** great cataclysms, great **cat**astrophes, which suddenly destroyed one condition of things and created another. Now most geologists are inclined to regard such changes as exceedingly gradual and protracted. In somewhat the same way, history is coming to be regarded not as made up of **a** number **of** decisive strokes by **a** series of great men, or of a number of great charters or constitutions, but as a slow growth and development. There do come times when a revolution seems to alter the face of society, when some constitutional change marks an epoch; but even then we cannot really understand the change unless we understand the previous causes, and the state of things which the change affected. Constitutional History thus understood is therefore, in the main, what the constitutional lawyer is apt to say it is not, "the steady growth of political changes," and not "occasional abrupt turns by organic amendment."

There is one other ambiguity to which we must refer before leaving the subject. The writer to whom I have already referred speaks of the legal conception of Constitutional History as itself inaccurate when compared with the *strict* sense of the term, which he thus defines:

"The aim of a Constitutional History is to give an account of the way in which the people of any country have governed themselves. This assumes that the people do govern themselves, that they form a nation, and that they are possessed of sovereign power. None but a self-ruling people can, in strictness, have a Constitution or a Constitutional History, because the meaning of the term constitution is the agreement or understanding whereby the whole people, the rulers and the ruled, choose to govern themselves."

This, you will see, is a special and derivative use of the word *Constitution*. Of course, there is nothing to prevent a writer from giving this meaning to the word, and confining himself to the history of very recent times in the great kingdoms and republics of Europe and America, with some occasional glances at ancient and mediæval republics, putting out of sight the history of the Roman Empire and nine-tenths of the history of modern Europe. But for our purpose,—to gain a true understanding of the forces at work in a political society,—this is insufficient.

Suppose we declare that Canadian Constitutional History begins properly in 1840. Can we understand from that even its present working? For instance, can we understand the relation of Quebec to the other provinces without some knowledge of the position therein of the Catholic Church; and can that be understood without reverting the circumstances of its establishment? Any such limitation of view is impossible for our purpose, and for us Constitutional History cannot be less than the whole political and social development of a people looked at in its relation to political organization.

Canadian Constitutional History, interesting as it is to all scientific students of politics of whatever country, demands especially the attention of those who care for Canada's future. Canada is not likely very long to remain exactly in its present position, but what is to become of it will very largely be determined by the working of its present Constitution. The existing Canadian Constitution may be roughly described as a combination of the political principles and machinery of England and the United States. Not that all in which Canada resembles England was borrowed consciously from England,—much of it was the natural growth in Canada of the same forces as produced in England the same results: nor that all in which Canada resembles the United States was consciously drawn from the United States,—much of it is the necessary outcome of Confederation. The Constitution of the United States was indeed, in its origin, as nearly a copy of the British Constitution of a hundred years ago as American statesmen could make under the circumstances. By this fact is to be explained the power of the President, and the separation and, to a large extent, independence one from another of the Executive and Legislature.* But during the next fifty years the Cabinet system was restored in England, after the interruption caused by the action of

* See Maine, *Popular Government*, Essay IV.

George III.; and the parliamentary **reform of** 1832 made the Cabinet dependent upon **a** majority **in** the House of Commons freely elected **by** the body of the people. **That such** changes had **taken** place is the reason why, when the **North American Colonies** obtained complete self-government in **1840, they received** an Executive dependent on the Legislature, and not one independent of it. The Canadian Senate, again, is a body which attempts to combine the principle **of** the upper **legislative** chamber, such as **exists in** France and England, **with** the principle of **safeguarding state,** *i. e.*, **provincial, rights,** as in the **United States.** **The discredit** which United States experience had cast upon an elected Judiciary, and the fact that after 1815 all suspicion attaching **to** the British Judges as partizans of the Government had passed away, combined **to give** Canada a Judiciary independent of popular **control.** And similar causes have prevented the introduction into Canada of **the** "spoils system." Moreover, while **in the Dominion Government** the very fact of Federation **has** introduced certain features similar to those of the United States Constitution, **the** Provincial political systems follow almost entirely the English, and not the American **pattern.**

To **the Englishman the Canadian** Constitution presents **the further interest that it is the first** attempt at Confederation **between a** group of British colonies. There are evident **signs that** the example will be followed before long by the colonies **of** Australia and South Africa.

Finally, to the scientific student of politics, the interest of Canada lies in the experiment which it is making in the combination of Cabinet government with a Federal system. The choice for nations in the future lies between the **American** and the British methods **of** organizing the Executive. It is not the **question** whether there shall be a President **or a** King, or what the Executive shall be called, but **it is the** question whether the Executive and

Legislature shall **be distinct or united.** There can be little doubt **that for a time the tendency** was towards the adoption of the American **plan.** Thus the President of the French Republic of 1848 was much more than a nominal figure head. He was to have independent **power**; he, and not his Prime Minister, was to be the **head of** the Executive. The dangers of such a system were illustrated by Napoleon's *coup d'etat*. The office of President, as created in 1871, was one much less powerful, but still powerful. But the Ministerial system is gradually making the French President a mere figure head. M. Floquet, not M. Carnot, is the real head of the French Executive. The further development of this question is what **constitutes** the interest of the Boulanger crisis.

And Canada **is not only** attempting Parliamentary government and Cabinet ministry, but it **is** combining it with Federation. And hence it occupies an almost unique claim on the attention of the student of political science. The only State which can offer a parallel is Austro-Hungary. **There also, there is a Federal** system; there also, the Ministers **are more or less** dependent on parliamentary support; and there also the situation is complicated by differences of race.*

---

* The best account in English of the Austro-Hungarian system will be found in Mrs. Birkbeck Hill's translation of Leger's *History of Austro-Hungary*.

LECTURE II.

On the Aristocratic Character of the Earlier Colonies.

AFTER what was said in the last lecture of the scope of Constitutional History, **you cannot expect** me to offer you anything worthy of the name. The Constitutional History of Canada has yet to be written; and it would be one of the happiest results of the establishment of this department in this University if it should induce one of you to turn his serious attention to the subject, and determine to supply this lamentable want. Mr. Bryce's great work on the American Commonwealth, though it is rather a description than a history of the political system, might serve as a model for the spirit in which the enquiry should be conducted; it will have rendered a great service to Canada if it induces Canadians to quietly take stock of their own position.

I do not purpose to give anything like a formal sketch of the history of Canadian **institutions.** I will not promise **even to introduce every date and fact** important for the examination. **You will find most of** them clearly enough **set forth in the first** sixty-two pages of Dr. Bourinot's manual. **I intend** rather to select some half a dozen topics, and to put **them in** the light in which, it seems to me, they may usefully be regarded.

First, then, let us look at the history of the old *régime* **in** French Canada. Most of the histories of Canada which **I have as yet** consulted give the impression that the aristo**cratic character of the** social organization of what is now the **Province of Quebec was** something altogether isolated and peculiar in the history of North America. I am not now referring to the absence until 1791 of anything like self-

government, and **the despotic** authority of the **French
King** acting through **the Governor and** Intendant during
the time it **was a** French province. Royal absolutism and
a feudal **social organization are by no manner of** means
necessarily connected. **Indeed it has been royal** absolutism
which everywhere in western **Europe,** and in consequence
in America, has succeeded **in destroying social feudalism,**
and **cleared the ground for the modern individualist, or, if
you** like, democratic society.

Feudalism **was rather** the great enemy **of monarchy;**
and the history of mediaeval Europe is full of feudal assemblies **or " estates"** which claimed to control the Sovereign
in legislation and taxation. Indeed, in one kingdom of
Europe, the kingdom of Poland, the national assembly of
Seigneurs **possessed so much power, that the government is**
more accurately **described as an aristocatic republic. There
was no Parliament, no Legislative Assembly in French
Canada, not because French feudalism was introduced, but
because French feudalism, with its** *Etats Generaux* **and its
provincial estates, was by that time half destroyed. You
will** remember **the last States General held in France**
before 1789 were those of 1614, **when the** *noblesse* **for the
last** time repeated their refusal to share in the burden **of**
national taxation. It was during the same period, **the
reign of Louis XIII.,** that the provincial assemblies, or
estates, **were also** deprived of the last vestiges of their
political power. **The** *seigneurie* was introduced into New
France, because with the existing social condition **of Old
France and** under **the** special circumstances **of** New
France **it was the only way of getting** Canada colonized at
all. But what I wish to point out is this, **that** what may be
called an *unfeudal* organization of society was not the rule
but the exception in the early history of the European
colonies in North America. Unfeudal is not a good word,
but it will serve for what is probably the usual modern
American ideal,—a society made up of a number of yeo-

men, or not over-large farmers, each taking part in the tilling of the soil and employing few men over and above the members of his own family,—a condition of things in which there is no large class of mere laborers, but also in which there are no over-lords, no great landlords, with tenants dependant upon them.

The only example of such a condition of things was in the New England colonies. It was not the condition of things in Virginia and the southern colonies of England ; it was not the condition of things in the Dutch colony of New Netherlands or New York ; and it was not the condition of things which men sought to establish in the unsuccessful colony of Nova Scotia or New Scotland. The New England colonies were exceptions, and exceptions due, as I shall afterwards explain, to a cause not elsewhere present—to religion. That such a semi-feudal system, as I have said was the rule in the early part of the seventeenth century, has not been established in the states and colonies founded during the eighteenth and nineteenth centuries, has been due not to any peculiarly English influence, still less to any peculiarly American influence, so much as to the fact that the decay of social feudalism had, in the interval, gone on rapidly both in Europe and America.

You may have been surprised at my mentioning the Southern Colonies of England in North America as characterised by aristocratic institutions. All of them had representative assemblies : Virginia we know, as early as 1619, had a House of Burgesses under the Constitution granted to it by its rulers, the London Company for Virginia; and we are told that James I. denounced the company itself as "a seminary for a seditious Parliament."* But the key to the situation lies in the one sentence of the historian which, in the account he gives of the democratic successes of the "few hundred sturdy liberty-loving Englishmen," is apt to be overlooked. "This year, marked in

* Lodge, *English Colonies in America*, p. 11.

Virginian annals by the *dawn of representative government and constitutional freedom,* is made still further memorable by the *introduction of the first slaves* in America." Where, indeed, were the men to come from who were to do the hard work of tilling the soil in these southern colonies? Not from the English farmers and yeomen, unless impelled by religious motives. They were tolerably comfortable in England, and felt no inducement to leave it. Were they to come from the rapidly increasing class of English agricultural labourers? They had not the money to transport themselves across the sea: there was no state-aided emigration then; and if they had been brought over by the "Merchant Adventurers," we may be sure it would not be in order that they might be settled down as independent yeomen. The difficulty was overcome by importing negro slaves, and English convicts, and "indented servants," who were little better than slaves;† and when we understand that all of the hard work of the southern colonies was done by slaves, the democratic liberties of their houses of assembly scarcely give Virginia a very clear superiority to feudal Canada. One of the best of American historians, Mr. H. C. Lodge, describing the condition of Virginia in 1765, has this sentence: "The men who formed the great mass of the white population of Virginia . . were good specimens of the nationality to which they belonged, and were a fine, sturdy, manly race, aristocratic in feeling, and, *from the ownership of slaves, despotic in temper;* but they were *earnest in the maintenance of English liberty.*"‡ To fairly judge French Canada, the economic position of "the habitant" must be compared, not with that of the farmers of the New

---

† For the first half of the seventeenth century the "indented servants" were the principal labouring class. "They were for the most part transported convicts, and the scum of the London streets. Many were kidnapped as children, as the trade was lucrative." *English Colonies in America,* p. 70.

‡ *Ibid.* p. 73.

England States, but with that of the negroes and "mean whites" of the South.

The Dutch gave modern Europe the first example of a powerful Republic, and it might be supposed that the growth of the commercial class in Holland, which secured for that country its commercial preeminence in Europe in the seventeenth century, would have been destructive to mediæval feudal traditions. Yet the Dutch West India Company, who took possession in 1621 of the territory of the New Netherlands, *i. e.*, New York as it became in 1664, found that, though their fur trade increased and became lucrative, colonisation did not prosper. The reason seems obvious; there was no sufficient inducement to the farmer class to emigrate, and no inducement was offered to the rich to pay for the transportation of the very poor.

The only way which the company could devise for overcoming this difficulty was the establishment of a feudal system; "the creation of what was intended to be a powerful and noble class. A charter was agreed to which gave any member of the company, *founding a colony of fifty persons*, the right to an estate with a river frontage of sixteen miles, and of otherwise indefinite extent, while with these estates went *every sort of feudal right including manorial courts*, and the privilege of trading within the dominions of the company. Leading directors promptly took advantage of this great opportunity."* The "patroon" system was afterwards largely modified; thus, in 1640, the company "restricted the patroons to a water front of one mile and a depth of two, but left them their feudal privileges." Settlers from English Colonies came in, and the organisation of society was still further affected by the introduction of negro slaves. Yet the early feudal institutions of New York long continued to exist over a large part of the state. "The most famous of these great estates" says Mr. Lodge, speaking of the middle

* *English Colonies in America*, p. 286.

of the eighteenth century, "was that of the Van Rensselaers, comprising all the territory in the neighborhood of Albany, peopled by farmers, and containing the thriving village of Rensselaerwyck; this manor, and those of the Cortlands and Livingstons, were each entitled to a representative in the Assembly. Besides these thus endowed with political privileges, there was the hardly less celebrated Philipse manor; and many leading families, principally of Dutch origin, such as the Schuylers, and Cuylers, owned or rented great tracts of land which they leased out to small farmers."* Speaking of the manor of the Philipses, which he tells us was a typical one, Mr. Lodge says, that "in the neighboring village, adjoining the manor house, the lord of the manor held once a year court leet and court baron, and meted out justice, sometimes in early days extending even to capital punishment. The relations between landlords and tenants became more and more unpleasant. There was wrong on both sides, and complaints of violence and extortion. Just before the Revolution riots broke out on some of the manors, the landlords were attacked, the sheriff fired upon, and finally the rising had to be suppressed by troops."

You probably know that seigniorial tenure was abolished in Canada in 1854. What is probably not so generally known is, that in "the Empire State," in the midst of all the rush of American business energy, seigniorial tenure was only abolished about eight years before, in 1846; and that until that date it existed over a considerable part of the state. A number of the Dutch families, especially the Van Rensselaers and Livingstons, continued to hold their estates under the feudal conditions. "The manor of Rensselaerwyck," we are told, "comprised a tract of country extending twenty-four miles north and south, and forty-eight miles east and west, lying on each side of the Hudson river. It was held by the tenants for perpetual leases.

* *English Colonies in America*, p. 327.

The rents were, on the Van Rensselaer estates, fourteen **bushels of** wheat for each hundred acres, and four fat hens, **and** one day's service with a cart and horses, to each farm of a hundred and sixty acres. Besides these there was a fine on alienation amounting to about half a year's rent." The reader **of Parkman** will **remember** all these incidents of land **tenure as** occurring in French Canada. In 1839, Stephen Van Rensselaer, the "patroon," died with great arrears owing **to** him, and his heirs proceeded to demand **payment.** Thereupon anti-rent clubs were formed to **return members** to the State Legislature who should **advocate their cause;** armed bands disguised as Indians **resisted the officers** in serving process; the militia were called out but in vain; and finally the Van Rensselaers and **Livingstons** were forced to sell their estates, "giving quit **claim deeds to the tenants** for what they chose to pay." Seigniorial tenure, therefore, far from being peculiar to **Canada, as** late as half a century ago was so strong in **New York** State that, as an observer said, it occasioned "a **reign of terror, which for ten** years practically suspended the operation of law and **the** payment of rent throughout the district."*

Another illustration of **the same** fact,—that unless men **were impelled by religious motives to** leave their own **country, a new land could be** "planted" in the seventeenth century **only by means of** a semi-feudal organisation, may be found in the **plan** for colonising "New Scotland" (Nova Scotia), adopted by James I. The documents relating to it will be found in a collection of *Royal Letters*, etc., relating to Nova Scotia, printed by the Bannatyne Club, in **1867.**

In **1621, Sir** William **Alexander, afterwards** Earl of Stirling, received a grant of the territory now forming the provinces of Nova **Scotia and New** Brunswick, with a

---

* See the quotation in Mr. Godkin's article in *Hand Book of Home Rule*, pp. 17-20.

commission of "Lieutenantry, Justiciary, and Admiralty."*
To obtain assistance for him in the work of colonization,
the King offered to all such "principal knights and esquires
as will be generously pleased to be undertakers of the said
plantation, who will promise "to set forth six sufficient
men, artificers or laborers, sufficiently armed, apparelled,
and victualled for two years,"† and will pay a certain
sum to Sir William Alexander for the surrender of portions
of his land, to confer upon them the title of Baronet,
together with a barony in New Scotland "three miles
long upon the coast and ten miles up into the country."‡
"Thus shall both those of the chief sort (avoiding the usual
contentions at public meetings), being by this hereditary
honour preferred to others of meaner quality, know their
own place at home, and likewise shall have their due
abroad."§

The project came to nothing, and the creation of baronets for Nova Scotia soon came to be nothing more than a means of raising money.‖ But this does not prove that there was no genuine intention to carry it out. Indeed, Sir William Alexander's son did equip a ship in 1627, and carry out a few men to Port Royal, in the Bay of Fundy, the site of the present Annapolis; and there was a Scotch settlement at this place until 1632, when, with other conquests, the place was surrendered to France.

The circumstances of New England were therefore peculiar. Its colonists were all men of much the same class,—yeomanry and small gentry: they came not that they might speedily become rich, as the tobacco planters of the southern colonies, but that they might establish their own form of religion; and they were sufficiently prosperous themselves to provide for the expense of the journey. They

---

* *Royal Letters*, 14.   † *Ibid*. 21.   ‡ *Ibid*. 18.   § *Ibid*. 17.

‖ The Nova Scotia Baronets had the honour of contributing a character to literature in the person of Sir Robert Hazelwood. *Guy Mannering*, ch. 42.

therefore naturally settled in yeoman fashion, as independent owners each of his own farm. To Canada no such class was tempted. The men who were at all likely to come of their own accord were the younger sons of nobles, seeking their fortunes. There was no hope of a labouring population, unless it were brought to the country at the expense of the government, of trading companies, or of individual adventurers: and if a labouring population were thus brought out, it seemed natural to subject them to a system which would compel them to labour, and so repay the cost of their plantation. Such a system was ready to the hands of the French Government in the form of land tenure and the relations dependent upon it, with which it was familiar at home.

LECTURE III.

On the Early Lieutenants General.

For the History of Canada under French rule there is abundant material, in the narratives of the men who themselves took a leading part in its colonization and government, the most important being that of Champlain, in the *Relations* of the Jesuits, in the reports of Intendants and Governors, in the edicts and ordinances of the home Government, and in the ordinances of the Intendants. Upon these have been based the valuable works of Parkman, and more recently of Mr. Kingsford. It is scarcely possible to speak too highly of the industry which has gone to the writing of these books. They have laid a foundation for the early History of Canada; Parkman bringing into relief its romantic side, and Mr. Kingsford coming after him with a somewhat cold and sceptical criticism of men and documents. For our present purpose, however, we cannot regard these works as final authorities, as anything more than material from which ourselves to form a judgment. Neither of them seems to me to regard the events of which they write in the dry light of absolute impartiality; both seem too much inclined to look at the events of the seventeenth century through the spectacles of the nineteenth. Mr. Parkman, in particular, is too serenely conscious of the superiority of modern common-sense American opinions over the "gaudy trappings of feudalism," and the "withering influences of monopoly." It is, one would hope, unnecessary to warn you against any imitation of his style, which may be called the laboriously picturesque. He is wont to proceed for a few pages with a smooth and vigorous narration; and then, without warning, comes some "purple patch" of rhetoric: "**Years rolled on:** France, long tossed among the surges **of civil commotion,** plunged at **last into a gulf** of patricidal war;" **or,** "One would **have thought him some** whiskered satyr, grim from the rack **of tumultuous years,"** a description of Henry **IV. of France.** This sort of thing, this turged rhetoric, is **easy** enough, "if **you** give your **mind to it;" and** that **is what makes it so** dangerous.

The **Constitutional** History of the Dominion **of** Canada may be said to begin **just** 290 years ago,—ten years before the **first** settlement **in " Canada " in the more** limited sense **of the word,**—with the patent granted in 1598 by Henry IV. to the Sieur de la Roche, creating him the royal Lieutenant-Governor in **the Countries of** Canada, Hochelaga, the New Lands (*i. e.* Newfoundland), Labrador, the River of the **Great** Bay of **Norembegue** (*i. e.* Nova Scotia, New Brunswick, and Maine), and the adjacent lands," with power of **" making** laws, statutes, **and** political ordinances" in the **countries** he should conquer; to enforce their observance, and punish or pardon offenders, as he may see good. His commission, **which is to be found in the** *Complément des Ordonnances* (published **at Quebec in 1803,** upon an address of the Chamber **of Assembly of Lower** Canada, and **reprinted in 1853), is of the** utmost importance. It con**tinues: "** In order **to increase the** good will, courage, and **affection of those who** shall take part in the expedition, and especially **of** those who shall dwell in the said lands, we have given **him** power to bestow the lands he may acquire to be enjoyed by the grantees and their successors, with all rights of property, to wit: to nobles (*gentilhommes*) **and** those he judges deserving, in fiefs, seigneuries, '*châtellenies*,' counties, viscounties, baronies, and other dignities **to** be held **of us (the king),** . . on condition that they shall serve in the defence of the country; and to others of lower estate, on such terms and with such annual payments as he may think fitting." The profits **of the enter-**

prise he is to divide into three parts: one-third for those who have assisted in the enterprise, a third for himself, and a third for the government or defence of the country. He is somewhat unnecessarily given the power to accept the assistance of such merchants and others as care to offer it, "but we expressly prohibit their trafficking without the knowledge and consent of our said lieutenant, on pain of the loss of their ships and merchandise." The patent is probably not much more than a copy of that granted to Roberval, the patron of Cartier, as long before as 1540: "We will that he shall have the the same power and authority as were granted by the late King Francis to the Sieur de Roberval."* But the little colony of Roberval and Cartier had maintained itself for only a couple of years: it had disappeared in 1543 or 1544. Since that time there had been almost certainly no settlement of persons staying over the winter on the mainland or islands of what is now called Canada; though two or three hundred fishing vessels came every year, chiefly from France, to the fisheries of Newfoundland, Cape Breton (which derives its name from the Bretons who then visited it), and Nova Scotia; and a small and hazardous fur trade with the tribes of Canada proper was intermittently maintained, with Tadoussac and Anticosti as its centres. But, from 1598, there was probably not a year in which Frenchmen did not remain encamped over the winter on Canadian soil; and from that year it is possible to trace a continuous line of trading companies and Royal lieutenants, with authority derived from the French King. Notice that the commission already brings into prominence two of the most important characteristics of the policy of the French Government toward New France: first, the monopoly of trade; and secondly, the

* I was not aware when I wrote this that the patent to Roberval is to be found in the *Notes pour servir a l'histoire etc. de la Nouvelle France* (Paris, 1872), 243 seq. The patent to De la Roche follows very clearly, as I had expected, and in most important particulars verbally, the earliest patent.

establishment of a colony based on the same social arrangements as existed in France.

Very little acquaintance with the history of France is **sufficient** to explain how it was that, for more than sixty years after the date of the patent to De la Roche, the French Government took no steps to ensure the colonisation of New France, and **left the** work of **exploration** and settlement entirely **to** private enterprise. **France had** but just come to the end of the Wars of **Religion, and it had** scarcely had breathing time **before** Richelieu **turned its** energies into a struggle with Austria and Spain in the Thirty Years' War, **while, in** addition to this, during part **of** the period, the country was also troubled by civil **war in the** disturbances of the Fronde.

During the period 1598-1627, the direction of colonisation and the control of trade in "New France" seems to **have** been, with scarcely an interval, nominally in the **hands** of some French **noble** or other, with **the** title of Lieutenant-General, by whom a monoply of trade was granted, now to two or three partners, now to a company. De la Roche made an unsuccessful **attempt to** establish a settlement in the **very year of his patent,** 1598, with no other result than **the abandonment on Sable** Island of **forty-four wretches given him from the** prisons, and the **removal of the eleven survi**vors to France in 1603.*
Meantime a couple of merchants, who had been given a monopoly **of the trade** on condition of establishing a colony of 500 persons,—whether the grant was from the King directly, or from De la Roche, it is hard to make out, though probably it was from De la Roche,—had made two successful voyages to the lower waters of the St. Lawrence in search of furs, and had attempted, though in vain, to estab-

* Such an abandonment of a new settlement was not infrequent ; and Bacon thought it necessary to remark in his Essay *On Plantations:* "It is the sinfulest thing in the world to forsake a plantation once in forwardness ; for, besides the dishonour, it is the guiltiness of blood of many commiserable persons."

lish a permanent trading settlement—like what was called in India, a *factory*—at Tadoussac. It was long before the French traders learnt to cope with **the Canadian** winter, and they were liable to starvation every year **if there were** any delay in the arrival of provision ships **from** France. In 1603 a company was formed, and Champlain was sent on a voyage of exploration, and went as far as Cartier had reached, to Hochelega, (or Montreal), where he found that the thriving Indian village described by his predecessor had already passed away. In 1604 a new Lieutenant-General, Des Monts, with the support of a still larger company of merchants, set about establishing settlements in Acadia, in the first instance on the island of St. Croix, at the mouth of the **river** of that name, the present boundary between New Brunswick and Maine : **it is interesting to find that part of the present frontier was actually determined** by the **discovery of the foundations of Des Monts'** buildings by **the boundary commissioners in 1798.** Next year the settlement was **transferred to the east side** of the Bay of Fundy, and the **year after, 1606,** to the very site of the present Nova Scotian Annapolis. Port Royal, or Annapolis, therefore, it seems to me, with the possible but doubtful exception of Tadoussac, is the place which can **most fairly** dispute precedence with Quebec as the site of the earliest permanent settlement in the Dominion. True, the place was **abandoned for** three years, 1607-1610, in consequence of a temporary withdrawal of the patent ; but when it was resettled in 1610, it was by the man, Poutrincourt, to whom Des Monts **had given a grant** of it, **and who had** first occupied it ; Poutrincourt, moreover, **had** made the first attempt to cultivate the land around during his earlier stay there, and he returned in 1610 to the dwellings he had left behind.

The suspension of trading monopoly in 1607 seems to have **been only** temporary ; it was regranted in 1608. But this **was sufficient to turn** the thoughts of Des Monts, and the merchants acting with him, in another direction. Champlain advised them to devote their attention to the establishment of a factory on the St. Lawrence. In Acadia, i. e., the Nova Scotia and New Brunswick of to-day, the Indian population was small, and the chances therefore of a successful fur trade inconsiderable; and there were in Acadia so many easily occupied harbors that the French could never be secure against the intrusion of other Europeans. **A factory on the** St. Lawrence might be made the centre **of a great trade,** and could more easily be defended. **Hence the** settlement of Quebec in 1608. **It was** with the same purpose, to secure the trade with the Indians of the Upper St. Lawrence, that in 1611, Champlain made a little encampment at Montreal. Between these two grew up the station at Three Rivers. From about 1612, therefore, we are to think of French settlements **at five** points,—at Montreal, Three Rivers, Quebec, Tadoussac, and Port Royal,—Tadoussac never more than a small trading factory, but of commercial importance for a long time quite as great as that of Quebec, as the centre for barter with the tribes of the north; and Port Royal, the first attempt, as we have seen, at colonisation, but at this time a separate **seigniory. In 1614, the** Port Royal **settlement was destroyed by the** English commander Argall: it was again occupied, and again conquered by **Kirke** in 1829. The son of Sir William **Alexander** attempted **to colonise** it with Scotchmen from 1629 **to** 1632, but the place was surrendered **by** Charles I. to France in 1632, and it remained in the possession of France till it was again conquered under Cromwell. It was restored once more by the Treaty of Breton, 1667; reconquered 1689; restored 1697 at the Peace of Ryswick; **and finally ceded to England at the Peace of U**trecht, 1713.

We may, for the present, leave the Acadian settlement on one side, and confine our attention to Canada in the more limited sense of the term. During the whole of the period from 1608 to 1627, the French population of the various factories, or "habitations," never exceeded two or three hundred. At Quebec, the permanent residents were not more than about 50, all in the employment of the fur traders, except a handful of priests and their servants. The trading monopoly changed hands occasionally; at one time it was held by a company of Norman and Breton merchants, at another by a couple of Huguenot merchants of Rochelle: in each case they obtained their grant, of course, for a consideration, from the Lieutenant-General, or "Viceroy," as he is sometimes called.

The office of Lieutenant was transferred by Des Monts, in 1612, to one of the more powerful French nobles, the Comte de Soissons; and after that it passed by Royal grant after a viceroy's death, or by purchase from a previous viceroy, to one magnate after another. But none of these, after Des Monts, made any attempt himself to go to Canada and found a settlement; they were contented with making the best terms they could with this or that group of merchants, and defending their interests at Court against the merchants who were excluded, or who refused to join the authorized company. The fur traders had no interest in promoting the colonisation of Canada: they would have been glad to have excluded all, save the men in their own employ. Their profits indeed were very considerable. Each year they brought home about 15,000 beaver skins, and they were at one time said to be paying an annual dividend of 40 per cent. Their payments to their protector, the Lieutenant-General, were large enough to make it on one occasion worth while to give as much as 11,000 crowns for the office. But if the Lieutenants-General did not go themselves, they must have some one to represent them and maintain some sort of government in Canada itself, and accordingly the viceroy, in 1612, made Champlain his representative, conferring on him all the political powers which he himself possessed, with the title of "Commandant," an office which was renewed by the successive **viceroys** until their rule was abolished. The two commissions printed in the volume *Complément des Ordonnances* are those of 1612 and 1625, and they are expressed in almost identical terms: "For the entire confidence we have in Sieur Samuel de Champlain, captain in the King's navy, and in his prudence and experience in naval matters, and the knowledge he has of the country from the voyages and visits he has made,—for these reasons, and in virtue of the power given us by His Majesty, we appoint, ordain, and depute **him to** be our lieutenant, to represent our person **in** the country of New France, and for this purpose **we** ordain that he shall take up his residence, with all his men, at the place called Quebec, being within the River St. Lawrence, otherwise called the great river of Canada, and at such other places as he may think fit:" he is there to build fortresses, to extend the knowledge of His Majesty's name, power, and authority, and to bring all the neighbouring peoples into subjection thereto; and in all lawful ways to lead them to the light of the Catholic faith. He is given power to appoint such officers as he pleases, "for the distribution of justice and the maintenance of **police** and good order;" to make treaties and alliances with neighbouring tribes, and to carry on war against them if necessary; to **promote** peaceable trade; and "for this purpose to make discoveries and expeditions in those lands, especially from Quebec, as **far as he** can up the rivers which flow into the St. Lawrence, to endeavour to find a road whereby it may be easy to journey to the country of China and the East Indies; and to search for gold, silver, copper, and other minerals. Finally, if he finds any persons, French or others, trafficking within the limits assigned to the viceroy, he is to seize them **and** take them to **France**, to be there judicially proceeded against."

You see that there is scarcely any suggestion here of a considerable settlement, or of the exercise of a regular government over a **French** population. Champlain's main function is, to protect the trading **stations, and secure the** monopoly of the merchants to **whom the** viceroy had granted it: if he likes to search for a passage to China, or to hunt for precious metals, like the Spaniards of Mexico and South America, he is permitted to do so; **but his chief duty is** that of the commander **of a** garrison. This is shewn by his title of *Commandant*, which **was usually** given in France to **the officer in** charge of **a garrison in a** fortified town.

In 1624, Richelieu had been called to the Council, and within **a few months** had made himself supreme. For some time his attention was too much engrossed by foreign affairs **to leave him time to consider** the position of Canada. But he **soon resolved that the** condition **of affairs in New France was unsatisfactory; and in 1627 he established a new system, which maintained itself for thirty-six years,** down **to 1663. The change consisted in the abolition of** the office **of viceroy, and the creation of a great company of** nobles, officials, **and traders, which should exercise both the political powers** previously **in the hands of the viceroy, and the** commercial monopoly. **In all the** early **colonial efforts of England and Holland,—I cannot speak of Spain —one of two plans was always adopted. Either a grant was made, conferring** political powers on **some one** *individual*, usually **a great** noble, or court favourite, who was then left to arrange **the government and trade of his new possession as he thought fit: this** was the early history **of** the so called *proprietory colonies*, **Maryland,** Pennsylvania, Carolina, **and Delaware ; it was, as we have seen,** the plan attempted by **James I. in regard to Nova Scotia ;** and such **was** the system **first** adopted **by the French** government in **relation** to Canada and Acadia. Or, and **this** was the favorite **procedure, a** charter was conferred upon a *company*, **which was given** both commercial monopoly, and political **power. The most notable English examples are** the London

Company for Virginia, chartered in 1606, which appointed the early Governors, and gave the colonists, after a few years, their representative system : the Governor and Company of Massachusetts Bay, chartered in 1609 : and above all, the English East India Company, chartered in 1600. But the example far more influential with Richelieu must have been that of Holland. During the war with Spain, the United Netherlands had become the foremost commercial power in Europe : and we shall see that the history of the second half of the seventeenth century is very largely made up of the struggle of England and France against Dutch commercial supremacy. This explains the wars of Cromwell and of Charles II. with the Dutch Republic. Now Holland had from the first adopted the expedient of chartered companies with both commercial and political powers. This was the case with the Dutch East India Company which, during the greater part of the century, was far more powerful than its English or French rival. Richelieu's attention, however, would be principally drawn to Dutch action in America. There, the New Netherlands had been founded in the first instance by a small trading company, with a monopoly : but after a few years the States General had taken away their privileges, and had conferred them on a new great Company of the West Indies, which was to have the same powers as the East India Company. It can hardly be doubted that Richelieu's creation of the *Company of the New France* (for that seems to be its more correct official title, and not the Company of a Hundred Associates) was directly prompted by the success of the Dutch experiment.

LECTURE IV.

Of the Company of New France, and *of the System of Government introduced in 1663.*

THE CHARTER under which Canada was ruled for twenty-six years, from 1627 to 1663, under which its colonization began, and a regular government was first established, deserves more attention than has hitherto been paid to it. It is the first of the documents in the *Edits et ordonnances royaux,* printed in Quebec in 1854.

It begins by declaring the two main objects of the government in establishing a colony,—to convert the natives, and to create a commerce beneficial to France. Of course it was desired that the new colonists should become as prosperous as possible ; but the success of the colony was not an end in itself, but a means to an end. It goes on to state that the previous recipients of royal patents had been so little anxious to bring about any such colonization, that up to the present, only one settlement had been formed ; Quebec, doubtless, is meant, shewing how small was the importance of Montreal and Three Rivers. This one settlement was only occupied, it says, by forty or fifty Frenchmen, who were there rather to look after the interests of the merchant than those of the King. Agriculture was so neglected that they were absolutely dependent on annual supplies from France. Accordingly, to the hundred members of a new company, is granted " *toute propriété, justice et seigneurie,*" full ownership, lordship, and jurisdiction, in New France, on condition that they take over two or three hundred men of all trades, in the next year, and 4000 in all of both sexes within fifteen years. The King, on his part, gave them a couple of ships ;

and it shews how little sanguine he was of the performance
of the stipulated conditions, that they were given ten years
out of the fifteen to take over 1500 persons, on pain of
forfeiting, on failure to do so, the value of the ships now
received. None but Catholics were to be taken out, and
the company were to maintain three priests in each settlement. Hitherto Huguenots had had a share in the commerce, at one time even monopolizing it ; and in one of
the early voyages to Acadia, the same ship had taken out
Catholic priests and Huguenot ministers, and had been the
scene of many disputes in consequence. The company was
to have a permanent monopoly of the trade in furs; and of
all other trade a monopoly for fifteen years : but the
Newfoundland cod fisheries were too much frequented
by Norman and Breton ships, to be handed over to
one company, and accordingly were excepted from its
authority. The government retained rather more control
over the government of the country than before : the
governor chosen by the company had to be approved of
by the government every three years ; and the company,
while they had the power to grant lands and titles, were
not to create baronies or higher degrees of nobility without the consent of the crown. Then follow the articles
of association, specifying the number of members, (Richelieu standing at the head of them, and, from his office of
Superintendent and Grand Master of the navigation and
commerce of France, having certain powers of supervision
over the company), the amount of individual shares, the
number of directors, the time of annual meeting, and the
like.

Under the new *régime*, Champlain was continued in his
office until his death in 1635, and he was followed by a
number of Governors and Lieutenants-General appointed
by the King on the nomination of the company, primarily
acting as commander of garrisons, but providing for such
other means of government as presented themselves.

The company could not begin its operations till 1632: for in 1629 the English took **Quebec, and held it** for three years. Mr. Kingsford is inclined to be angry with Charles I. for the cession of his conquest. He seems to think that if the English government had **determined to retain** it, it would have been colonized by Englishmen, and there would have been no French nationality in Lower Canada. It is never particularly useful to speculate on what might have been. It is, for example, very probable that had **England** retained it in 1632, France would have reconquered it during the troublous times of the English civil wars; for Richelieu would by no means have readily consented to the loss of prestige which such a defeat of his colonial policy would have involved. But, granting that it had remained an English possession, it is very probable that it would **have remained unoccupied** by settlers down to the time of the **U. E. Loyalists.** Seeing how small was the emigration **from New England to Nova** Scotia and New Brunswick down to that period, **it is** very doubtful whether any considerable number of **colonists** would have gone across the St. Lawrence. There **was no inducement to** English yeomen or labourers to leave England for Canada. What would probably have taken place is, that Canada would have been handed over to a trading company, which would have done as little to settle the land as the Hudson Bay Company did in the North West.

To return to the company of New France. They retained their powers until 1663; with the result that the **French population at the end of that time was, at most, 2,500, and** that the colony **was hourly threatened with** destruction by the Iroquois. The first **seigneury dates** from 1634; in that year M. Gifford having received a grant at Beauport, six miles from Quebec, brought over a number of artisans and country labourers, and founded the first Canadian village. But his example was followed by but two or three. In fact the offer of a seigniory, with however wide a territory, was not sufficient inducement to bring French adventurers over, when they had to provide for the transportation of the men who were to till the fields, to provide for their maintenance for the first year, and to provide for their protection against the Iroquois. The trading monopoly was relaxed in 1645 and 1648. What exactly took place is not clear, but it would seem that the inhabitants were given permission to take part in the fur trade, on condition of bearing some part of the expenses of government and of the maintenance of 100 soldiers. But after a short interval, during which the company contented itself with exacting the annual payment of 1,000 furs, it fell back on its monopoly of the trade with Europe, and the colonists were obliged to sell their furs to the agents of the company at a fixed price. Somehow or other, the trade had fallen, by 1663, into the hands of a little ring at Quebec, who excluded the rest of the inhabitants and defrauded the company.

In the constitutional history of the period, in the narrow sense of the term, the most important fact is the gradual growth of a *Consultative Council* around the Governor, composed of the chief ecclesiastic, the local governor of Montreal, when he could be present, and the syndics, or municipal chiefs, of the three settlements.

Of far more real importance, however, are the beginnings of the ecclesiastical system, and the struggle with the Iroquois. Champlain, whether wisely or not, had joined the Hurons in their war with the Iroquois. He cannot have been aware,—he had no opportunity to learn,—of the relative strength of the two powers. But the Iroquois had already become far the stronger, and the interference of the French, unable to contribute a force which could be of any real assistance to their allies, did but hasten the annihilation of the Hurons, and almost brought about the destruction of the French settlement also. The danger in which the colony stood was one of the main causes which induced the Home Government to take the defence and settlement of Canada into its own hands, in 1663. As the King declares in a document printed in *Edits et Ordonnances*, p. 32, "instead of learning that the country was peopled, as it ought to be, considering the long time our subjects have been in possession of it, we have learnt with regret that, not only is the number of the inhabitants very small, but also that they are in daily peril of being driven out by the Iroquois, a danger against which a remedy must be provided; and considering that this company of a hundred men is almost destroyed by the voluntary withdrawal of the majority of its shareholders, and that the few who remain are not strong enough to support the colony, and to send the forces and men necessary either for colonising or defending it, we have resolved to withdraw it from the hands of the said shareholders."

We have seen that the grant of 1627 to the Company of New France excluded from Canada all but Catholics, and created an established Church by stipulating that the company should support three priests in each settlement. Mr. Parkman laments the exclusion of the Huguenots, and contrasts the policy of the French Government with that of England, "which threw open the colonies to all who wished to enter." Now, when we consider how valuable an element in the French nation were the Huguenot craftsmen, how much France lost and England gained by their expulsion from France in later years, it is natural for a Protestant to regret that a Huguenot Colony did not spring up in Canada. But to judge the policy of the French Government properly, several things have to be kept in mind. In the first place, it is a misleading figure of speech to talk of England throwing open her colonies to all who wished to enter. To use such a phrase to the Pilgrim Fathers would indeed have astonished them. The English Government allowed Puritan Colonies to grow up in New England very much because it could not help it. Secondly, it must be remembered that the principle of toleration was at this time no more recognised by the Huguenots than it was by the Catholics. It is a common mistake to credit the Puritans with modern ideas of toleration, and to speak as if all they sought in the New World was liberty to serve God in peace in their own way. As a matter of fact, it was long before the mass of the Puritans learnt toleration from their own sufferings; and when the principle of absolute toleration was at last asserted, some years after this time, it came from the extreme section of the Independents, the despised Anabaptists. As of course you know, a very rigid establishment of religion took place very early in the New England Colonies, and dissenters from it were barbarously punished. In the same way, the Huguenots would not have been content merely with permission to exercise their religion as they pleased; and the young colony would have been torn asunder by two religious parties, each endeavouring to make its religion the established one. And thirdly, though there was a great body of quiet, industrious Huguenots in Southern France, what the name Huguenot chiefly meant to the French Government was a party of self-seeking nobles, who made use of the pretext of religion to enrich themselves, and secure semi-independence. There had been repeated Huguenot rebellions in recent years, and at the very time that the charter of the Company of New France was being signed, the Huguenots had joined hands with a foreign enemy, England, and Richelieu was engaged in the great siege of Rochelle.

Until 1663, however, the efforts of the Church in Canada took an almost exclusively missionary direction. It was for some time a question whether the evangelisation of Canada should fall to the Recollets, a branch of the Franciscans, or to the Jesuits; but the Jesuits were able to secure the Royal favour, and from the restoration of Quebec to the French, in 1632, the missions of Canada were almost **entirely in their hands.** Their only rivals were the Sulpician **fathers at Montreal.** In 1640, the Company of New **France had ceded** "all rights of ownership, lordship, and justice," **over part of** the Isle of Montreal, to be held of them in fief, to a society formed **like an** ordinary mercantile company, entitled, "The Gentlemen Associated for the Conversion of Savages at Montreal,"—a number **of** enthusiasts, many of them laymen of high rank, who subscribed their money for the purpose of founding a religious settlement. The settlement began in 1642; in 1659 **the** Company of Montreal was given the rest of the island. In 1644, they had obtained the right of naming their own Governor,* and of administering justice; with this limitation, however, that there should be an appeal from the Montreal Judges **to** the Governor of Quebec. In later years these **rights were transferred** from the company to the Fathers of **the great Seminary of** St. Sulpice, at Paris, with which **its members had been** closely **connected.** The seminary became **a great feudal lord, and** Montreal not infrequently the **centre of opposition to** the Jesuits of Quebec. But, until **1663,** the colony at Montreal was extremely small, and had the greatest difficulty in maintaining itself against the Iroquois.

I **have** worked out in some detail the constitutional history **of** Canada in its earliest years, because it is disregarded **in the ordinary** books. The constitution, established in **1663 and remaining down to** 1763, is sufficiently well described **in Mr. Bourinot's** valuable work, and **it is unnecessary here to speak of it in** detail. The **first duty of** the Government **was** to defend **the country from the** Iroquois; and **a** Royal regiment **of** regulars, **sent over** under an extraordinary high official,—the "Viceroy for America," M. de Tracey,—inflicted such losses upon them that the country enjoyed peace for twenty years. Then M. de Tracey withdrew, though a large part of the regiment

* *Edits et Ordonnances,* p. 25.

remained and became settlers. The administration was henceforth in the hands of the Governor, the Intendant, and a Supreme, or, as it was afterwards called, a Superior Council, consisting of these two together with the Bishop, or chief ecclesiastic in the country, and first five, then seven, and finally twelve other members, chosen from the inhabitants after 1675 (up to which time a new trading company, the Company of the West Indies, had nominated them), by the King on the recommendation of the Governor or Intendant. It is usual to say that the change in 1663 consisted in assimilating Canada to a French province. This is in the main, true, and it is especially illustrated by the position of the Governor and Intendant. The Council, in so far as it exercised supreme judicial authority, resembled the great provincial "Parliaments," and like the French Parliaments, it was obliged to register the edicts sent over to it by the home government. But there were several important differences. The French Parliaments were composed of lawyers holding their position by hereditary right; the Canadian Council was composed of merchants and seigniors. Moreover, another great difference : the Council exercised very considerable powers of legislation, such as were only exercised at home by the King in Council. So that it is hardly accurate to speak of the Canadian government as a mere reproduction of the home government, and as in everything dependent on the arbitrary will of the King. Of course, the King did occasionally interfere, but in the main, the administration was carried on by the Governor and Intendant, with the aid of this Council of residents ; so that, to use modern language, the government was much more "liberal" than that at home. I suppose it is possible that during this period, a representative assembly might have been of some advantage to the country, though I am not at all sure of it. In the Council there was, of course, room for self seeking and peculation ; but the nomination of the members was in the hands of a Governor and an

Intendant, neither of whom resided in the country long enough to become very much involved in local family interests; and the Intendant, in particular, an official on his promotion, was anxious to stand well with the home authorities, and therefore, to secure a decent government for the country to which he was sent. It is interesting to notice that in 1676, one of the very few occasions on which a popular assembly, a gathering of the chief inhabitants of Canada, was consulted, they voted almost unanimously for unrestricted trade in brandy with the Indians: a trade which Laval and the Jesuits were straining every effort to destroy, and which the Council itself sometimes plucked up courage enough to prohibit.*

A word now as to the Governor and Intendant. The Governor had official precedence, and was regarded as the especial representative of the King's person. But his main function was that of commander of the military forces. It was not the policy of the government to deprive him altogether of political power; but the Intendant was given a preponderating authority in matters of justice and police, and presided over the deliberations of the Council. The office of Intendant had gradually grown up in France during the religious wars of the second half of the sixteenth century. At first the Intendants were merely temporary commissioners attached to the armies; then they were sent to certain provinces to inquire into the collection of revenue and the administration of justice. From the accession of Richelieu to power, they became regular permanent officials in every province, for the purpose of controlling the Governor who was usually a great noble, and ready to seize every opportunity to make himself independent.† Gradually one after another of the

* Parkman, *Old Régime in Canada*, ch. 18.

† The early history of the office of Intendant has only recently been worked out by M. Hanotaux, in the *Revue Historique*, 1882-3. A summary of his conclusions will be found in Gasquet, *Precis des Institutions de l'Ancienne France*, part i., chap. iii.

powers of the Governors was transferred to them, until by the time of the French Revolution, the office of Governor was scarcely more than a titular honor. The Intendants belonged to the class of lawyers and officials; they were absolutely dependent upon the Royal Council, and the instruments of its centralising policy. For New France, this need of centralisation was not so strongly felt, and there was but little danger of the Governor creating an independent principality. On the other hand, the circumstances of the country, and especially the constant danger of attack from the Indians, made it necessary that there should always be in the country a nobleman accustomed to command armies, and that he should be entrusted with a wider authority than would have been given him at home.

Then, as to the establishment of the seigneurial system. For those who have read Parkman's Old Régime, it is not necessary that I should describe the method by which the colonisation of Canada was secured. What Parkman, however, does not clearly bring out is, that this colonisation was entirely the work of the French government, and involved an enormous expenditure of money. Notice first how rapidly the population increased. In 1663, it was 2,500; within a couple of years it was 3,215; in 1667, 4,300; in 1668, 5,870; and in 1679, 9,400. From that time the increase was slower, because the home government was obliged, by the European wars, to withdraw its aid. Until 1672, hundreds of colonists were taken out every year by the King's ships, and supplied with every necessary for entering upon their new life. At the same time, large sums were spent in assisting those who were already in Canada to marry, and bring up large families. But the government could devise no better way to secure the cultivation of the land by those it had borne the expense of taking thither, than by conferring tracts in seigniory on the gentilhommes, on pain of forfeiture, if the land was not cultivated, and empowering them to do the same to vassals, on the same conditions. Yet it by no means abandoned the "habitant," the "censitaire," to the tender mercies of the seigneur; the Intendant and the Royal Council at home were his watchful guardians, and frequently interfered to modify the conditions of his tenure. Most of the seigneurs were miserably poor, and forced to work in the fields like their tenants, until increasing population and prosperity in the eighteenth century altered their relative positions.

Finally, as to the establishment of the Roman Catholic ecclesiastical system. You doubtless know that it was by Laval that the parochial system of Old France was established in Canada; with this important difference, however, that Laval insisted on making the curés removable by the bishop, and without that sort of freehold in their office which they possessed at home. And you know that it was Laval who introduced the payment of tithes,—at first a thirteenth, and subsequently a twenty-sixth. But there are one or two points on which stress must be laid. *First*, that there were no such scandals in Canadian ecclesiastical administration as appeared in France: the money drawn from the inhabitants by tithe or contribution was honestly and economically spent. *Secondly*, that the ecclesiastical revenue derived from Canada was utterly inadequate to maintain its clergy, and that during the whole of its history a large part of the cost of maintaining them was borne by the home government,—for the first half of the period, far the larger part: and, *Thirdly*, that the church contributed more than any other agent to the creation of an orderly and thrifty population, overcoming in the main the tremendous temptations presented by the fur trade, and the brandy trade bound up with it. "The most orderly and thrifty part of Canada," says Parkman, speaking of 1683, "appears to have been at this time the Côte of Beaupré, belonging to the Seminary of Quebec. Here the settlers had religious instruction from their curés, and industrial instruction also, if they wanted it. Domestic spinning and weaving were practised at Beaupré sooner than in any other part of the country." His final judgment,—the judgment of a not over-friendly critic,—is this: "The ecclesiastical power, wherever it had a hold, was exercised with an undue rigour: yet it was the chief guardian of good morals; and the Colony grew more orderly and more temperate as the Church gathered more and more of its wild flock within its fold."

LECTURE V.

On the Expulsion of the Acadians.

A NATURAL result of the preponderance of the two old Canadas, Upper and Lower, in the Dominion, and also of the fact that the Constitutional History of Canada has hitherto engaged the attention chiefly of natives of those particular provinces, has been that the political development of the Dominion has been looked at too exclusively from the point of view of Quebec or Toronto. We are given the history of French Canada down to 1763; the growth of an English population in Upper Canada; the consequent difficulties in the relations of the two nationalities; the struggles leading up to 1867; and then the historian turns aside for a moment to give some brief account of Nova Scotia and the other provinces which, in 1867, or subsequently, entered into confederation. It seems to me, however, that another method of treatment might with advantage be sometimes adopted. We have first to trace the colonization and organisation of New France. But scarcely had this old Canada been withdrawn from the hands of a trading company, a population carried over to it and planted on the soil, and an orderly civil government established, when, in the country to the North West, upon the Hudson Bay, appeared another trading company, and this time an English one, which was destined to maintain itself, with but brief intervals, during which it succumbed to the fortunes of war, until our own time. Yet, though the Hudson Bay Company was founded as early as 1670, no colonization of the territory it ruled took place until the present century. If we turn, however, in the other direction, we find in Nova Scotia a

British government permanently established from **1713** onward : and a Legislative Assembly established in 1758, a year before the English took Montreal, thirty-three years before there was any other elected Legislative Assembly in what is now British North America. From 1598 to **1670** then, we need have French **Canada** alone before our minds; from 1670 to 1713 we have to think of the French province and the English trading company side by side; from 1713 onward, an English colony in Nova Scotia is added to the picture,—a colony which **first of** those now forming the Dominion became self-governing. 1784 added another element in **New** Brunswick, 1791, another in Ontario; 1858, another in British Columbia; until all these diverse strands **are** at last brought together in the unity-in-diversity of confederation.

Perhaps it will be replied that a view such as this is **mere** historical pedantry : that the fact that all these **provinces** now form part of the Dominion is no reason for supposing that there is any fundamental unity in the forces by which their fates have been and will be determined. Whether there be such a unity **or no,** events alone can shew. But while **the Dominion lasts, it** certainly seems to be more fitting to regard its constitutional **history as a number of parallel** streams which at last **converge, rather than as** one stream which has received **a number of tributaries.**

Nova Scotian constitutional history, however, demands more attention **than it** has hitherto received from Ontario, for reasons stronger even then these. The shape taken by the Confederation, and its subsequent history have been to **no** small degree the work of Nova Scotian statesmen; and **this being** so, it is not really possible even to understand **Confederation** and later development without some knowledge **of the** political history of a province which has had a longer experience of representative government than any other. We must be satisfied for the present, however, to work at the earlier **stages of** this history.

We are fortunate in having at our disposal a convenient collection of the more important documents relating to the period 1713-1761, in the volume known as *Nova Scotia Archives*, or, to give it its full title, *Selections from the Public Documents of the Province of Nova Scotia*, prepared and published in 1869, at the expense of the Provincial Government, in accordance with a resolution of the House of Assembly, and edited by Dr. Akins, the Commissioner of Public Records. I have already spoken of the collections of documents relating to French Canada made at the instance of the Government of Quebec. Ontario, so far as I am aware, has no Government publications to show which can compare with these. Its history is, of course, briefer, and the events to which it owes its birth are more recent. But they have already passed far beyond the limits of living memory. Nothing could be more useful to the student of Ontarian constitutional history than the publication by the Ontarian Government of a handy collection of the official papers relating to the settlement of the U. E. Loyalists; and such a work should especially commend itself to a Government which is certainly not disposed to overlook the fact that the Province has had an independent life and growth of its own, apart from the Dominion. The way has already been in part prepared by the valuable collection of MSS. brought together by the Chief Librarian of the Toronto Public Library.

In another direction Ontario compares unfavourably with other Provinces. For the history of New France and its conquests, much has been done by the Historical Societies of Quebec and Montreal; for that of the Maritime Provinces, by the admirable collections of the Nova Scotia Historical Society; but nothing of the like has yet been done in Ontario.

We have seen that Acadia, or Nova Scotia, was finally ceded to England by France at the Peace of Utrecht, in 1713. The numbers of the French-speaking and Catholic

Acadian population at that date have been variously estimated. One of the English military commanders reckoned them at 2,500, or 500 families.* A more detailed account drawn up in 1720, tells us that they were almost all grouped in four considerable settlements along the eastern shores of the Bay of Fundy: on the Atlantic coast there were but a few scattered families. The four settlements were: (1) at Annapolis, or Port Royal, where were "a great many fine farms on both sides of the river, inhabited by about 200 families;" (2) at Manis, or les Mines, where the inhabitants were "more numerous" than in the Annapolis district; (3) at Cobequid, where were "about fifty French families;" and (4) at Chignecto, "about seventy or eighty families."† This would give a population of over three thousand, to which must be added the scattered population of the Atlantic shore. The question which the British Government had to decide was, what was to be done with these Acadians. Most of them were anxious to leave the country and settle in Cape Breton, which remained a French possession. The French Government was doing what it could to make Cape Breton a bulwark of French power, and a centre from which it could renew the struggle for the possessions it had lost. The strong fortifications of Louisbourg were being erected; and immigrants from the old French provinces were offered "eighteen months provisions," and assistance "with ships and salt to carry on the fishery."‡ The French inhabitants of Newfoundland were permitted to accept the offer: but the English Government could not make up its mind to let the Acadians follow their example. The commander, before quoted, reported to the English " Lords of Trade " :—

"The consequences of the French moving from Nova Scotia to Cape Breton . . are evidently these. There

* *Nova Scotia Archives* 5.

† *Description of Nova Scotia*, by Paul Mascarene, *ibid.* 39 *et seq.*

‡ *Nova Scotia Archives*, 5.

being none but French and Indians (excepting the garrison) settled in those parts, and as they have intermarried with the Indians, by which and their being of one religion they have a mighty influence upon them; so it is not to be doubted but they will carry along with them to Cape Breton both the Indians and their trade, which is very considerable. And as the accession of such a number of inhabitants to Cape Breton will make it at once a very populous colony (in which the strength of all the countries consists) so it is to be considered that one hundred of the French, who were born upon that continent and are perfectly known in the woods, can march upon snow shoes, and understand the use of birch canoes, are of more value and service than five times their number of raw men newly come from Europe. So their skill in the fishery, as well as the cultivating of the soil, must inevitably make that island by such an accession of people, and French, at once the most powerful colony the French have in America. And of the greatest danger and damage to all the British colonies as well as the universal trade of Great Britain."*

Accordingly the English government determined to refuse permission to them to depart, and to put every obstacle in the way of their leaving the country; but it took pains to make their enforced residence as little of a hardship as possible. To win their confidence, in the first place they were left untaxed. In the second place, they were given a sort of representative local government, which is thus described by Haliburton † : "They were required to choose annually in their separate parishes, deputies to act on their behalf, and to publish the orders of the governor. For this purpose, the settlements on the Annapolis river were divided into eight districts, which chose each one deputy, and the other more extensive divisions of the province severally elected

* *Nova Scotia Archives*, 6; cf. for other reasons, 41.
† *History of Nova Scotia*, i., 96.

four. These deputies, twenty-four in number, were annually chosen on the tenth day of October. They were authorized to act as arbitrators in small matters of controversy between the inhabitants, and from their decision an appeal was allowed to the Governor and council. For the hearing of these appeals the council sat three times a year. On these occasions the inhabitants generally pleaded their own causes, assisted by an interpreter." But what might have been supposed most likely to conciliate the new subjects was, the religious liberty allowed to them in accordance with the provisions of the Treaty of Utrecht. The ecclesiastical arrangements which had grown up in Acadia were left unchanged. The only limitation which was imposed was an order which ran as follows : " When any missionary causes a vacancy by death, or by withdrawing from the province, the inhabitants of the parish must apply for leave to send for another, and when upon such permission a missionary arrives, he is not to settle or exercise his functions till, by repairing to Annapolis, he has obtained the approbation of the Commander in Chief, and is directed to his parish ; and no missionary thus appointed is to remove to another parish without leave."* But some such check on the *personnel* of the clerical body was absolutely necessary from the point of view of British interests. The priests sent by the ecclesiastical superiors in French Canada were only too likely to be, and certainly frequently were, political agents as well as spiritual pastors. The whole arrangement, however, was remarkably liberal when we consider the state of the penal law in England itself at this time. An Act of 1699, which was still unrepealed, made Catholic priests, convicted of celebrating mass or discharging any sacerdotal function in England, liable to perpetual imprisonment. Moreover, according to other statutes, all persons who refused to take the oath of supremacy (which no conscientious Catholic could take)

* Quoted in Haliburton, *Ibid.* note.

when tendered to them by **two justices of the** peace, became incapable of inheriting or purchasing land, and their property passed to the next heir. **Of course,** these statutes were evaded, and **the** government refused to put them into execution. **But it** did not **dare to** repeal them. Yet, as has not infrequently been the case, it was more liberal than the nation it represented, and wherever it had a **free hand** this greater liberality **was** always displayed. **It often** repealed **Acts** passed in the colonies imposing **civil disabilities** on Dissenters, while such disabilities still existed at **home.*** And here we see it, as later in the more important case of Canada, openly permitting the exercise of the Roman Catholic religion.

But in **spite of** these **concessions, the Acadians** persistently refused to take **the oath of allegiance to the** English Crown. **At first they tried to escape from taking the oath under any conditions; but after a few years they so far** yielded, as **to consent on condition that they were expressly** exempted from the obligation **to bear arms,** *i. e.*, to fight against **the French. On one or two occasions, the** local representative of the **government,** in 1726 even the Lieutenant-Governor, yielded to this request. **In the year** just mentioned, the Lieutenant-Governor assured them that, "it being contrary to the laws of Great Britain that a Roman Catholic should serve in the army," they need not fear lest they **would be called** upon to fight, but this verbal explanation not **satisfying them,** "the Governor with the **advice** of the council **granted the** same ["a clause whereby they **may** not be **obliged to carry arms"] to be writ** upon the margin **of the French translation, in order to** get them over by **degrees."*** **Such a qualified** promise of allegiance the home government refused to accept. In 1730, Governor Phillips seemed to be more successful and secured from the inhabitants of the Annapolis River, an unconditional oath. But My Lords Commissioners for Trade and

* Lecky, *History of England*, iii., 273. † *Archives*, 67.

Plantations were by no means satisfied. They pointed out to the disappointed Governor that the oath was far too vague, and that owing to a want of attention to French idiom, it conveyed a promise to *obey* King George without a promise to be *faithful* to King George.* But the French inhabitants could never be induced to take a more satisfactory oath. The position they considered themselves to occupy was expressed in the term they applied to themselves, the "neutrals,"—a position not unnatural for a people who had been handed over from one ruler to another by the fortunes of war, but which no sovereign of that age was likely to recognize. And so matters dragged on. The Acadians increased in numbers at a rate which added to the alarm of the English Governors, who had only a small force at their disposal : for it must be remembered that no English immigration took place until 1749. Additional causes of irritation and suspicion were not wanting. The Governor and council had attempted to decide the cases brought before them by English law, while, as the Governor complained in 1732, "the French here upon every frivolous dispute plead the laws of Paris, and from that pretended authority contemn all the orders of the government."† This experience of the difficulty of imposing an alien system of law upon a conquered people was probably not forgotten when forty years later a different policy was decided upon in the case of Canada.

* The oath ran " *Je promets et jure sincerement en foi de chrétien que je serai entirement fidele, et obeirai vraiment sa majesté le Roy George le Second, que je reconnoi pour le souvrain seigneur de l'Accadie ou Nouvelle Ecosse. Ainsi Dieu me soit en aide.* My Lords Commissioners point out that "the particle 'to' in the English oath being omitted in the French translation, it stands a simple promise of fidelity without saying to whom . . and it is to be feared that the French Jesuits may explain this ambiguity so as to convince the people upon occasion that they are not under any obligation to be faithful to his Majesty." *Archives*, 84.

† *Ibid.* 94.

A source of graver discontent was present in the religious difficulty. The French missionary priests were in part maintained by pensions from the French King; and this the English government, curiously enough, seems to have been willing to allow.* But, under such circumstances, they were not unlikely to do what they could to keep alive the French sympathies of their flocks, and even to act occasionally as the agents of secret negotiations. The English Governor naturally tried to keep them under a careful supervision, and for this reason insisted on the rule which had been laid down when the province passed into British hands, namely, that no priest should take charge of a parish without his approbation.† We find him complaining to the home government, as early as 1732, that the Roman Catholic ecclesiastical authorities in Canada set this rule at defiance: "the bishop of Quebec orders not only the building of churches here, but sends whom and what number of priests he thinks proper;"‡ and "the inhabitants of the province," he writes on another occasion, "are more subject to our neighbours of Quebec and those of Cape Breton than to His Majesty, . . being entirely governed by their most insolent priests, who for the most part come and go at pleasure, pretending for their sanction the Peace of Utrecht."§ Ten years later we find the bishop of Quebec sending a couple of priests into the Province without consulting the Governor, and conferring on one of them authority, as grand vicar, over the Catholic clergy in Nova Scotia.‖ The increase of the Acadian population probably made necessary a larger clerical body, and the establishment of a local ecclesiastical authority; but it is probable that the bishop of Quebec and the priests he sent were not particularly careful to avoid offending the English Government in Nova Scotia, just as it is probable that the British Government, in its constant dread of an Acadian revolt, were sometimes

* *Archives*, 105. † *Ibid.* 122, 124. ‡ *Ibid.* 95. § *Ibid.* 101. ‖ *Ibid.* 121-126.

unnecessarily high handed in their repressive methods. It is to be noticed that their efforts to introduce English law instead of French, had had the effect of increasing the influence of the priests over their people; unwilling to have recourse to the Council and English law, the parishioners brought their complaints before the priest. "The priest examines the neighbour in the way of confession. The man denies his owing or detaining such a thing unjustly. The priest does not stop where he should, but calls and examines witnesses, and then decides in a judicial manner, and condemns the party to make restitution, and to oblige him thereto refuses to administer the sacraments. . Consider how this tends to render all civil judicature useless."*

It was indeed a miserable situation, a situation for which the blame cannot be laid upon any one in especial of the parties concerned, but which was the natural result of circumstances. The one underlying cause was the state of public morality which permitted a people to be transferred against their will to an alien rule. But this was a fault common to all the great powers of the eighteenth century, to France as well as to England.

For the rest of the story, down to the removal of the Acadians in 1755, I would refer you to the fourth and eighth chapters of Parkman's *Montcalm and Wolfe*. The difficulties which shewed themselves in the Government of Nova Scotia during the long peace between England and France which followed the Peace of Utrecht, may fairly perhaps be regarded as inherent in the situation. But there cannot be the slightest doubt, since the publication of the documents on which Mr. Parkman bases his narrative, that during the next great struggle between England and France for the possession of the American continent, the French Government secretly used the Acadians as tools, encouraged them, through their agents the

* Letter of Governor Mascarene, 1741, *ibid.* 111.

missionaries, in their refusal to accept English rule, and hoped to make use of them in a final attempt to recover the peninsula. In reading the whole pitiful story, our indignation is enlisted on behalf of the miserable Acadians against the French Government, as much as, or more than, it is afterwards aroused against the English. During 1751-3, the Vicar-General Le Loutre, in order to increase the strength of the French position in Cape Breton and the Isle St. Jean, compelled between three and four thousand of them to abandon their homes under threats of attack from the Indians under his control; and the miseries caused by this migration were hardly less than those which afterwards attended the removal of the rest of the population by the English Governor. Earlier even than that, Le Loutre had forced the Acadian inhabitants of Beaubassin to pass over to the French side of the River Missaquash, and join the French forces around Beausejour, by the simple process of burning their village.

Such was the position of affairs when, in 1755, the final struggle between England and France for the the New World was seen to be imminent. In the capture of Beausejour some three hundred Acadians were found among its defenders. The inhabitants of the Acadian settlements along the Bay of Fundy had, but a few years ago, absolutely refused to take an unqualified oath of allegiance, and it was suspected, as we now know was indeed the case, that the refusal was prompted by the agents of the French Governor of Cape Breton, and enforced by threats of vengeance at the hands of the Micmac disciples of the missionaries. Any day a French fleet might come up the Bay of Fundy, and a rising of the Acadians, assisted by the fleet and by aid from Canada and Cape Breton, might easily overpower the small English colony at Halifax—of which I shall say something hereafter. The New England volunteers, who had come to the assistance of the English Governor, would soon be returning; and the Governor,

Lawrence, resolved to give the Acadians one more opportunity to make their peace, and if they refused to take it, to get rid of them. Once more the oath was offered to them, once more it was refused, and then the provincial government decided on their forcible removal.

This was in 1755-6. The act was a harsh one, and excused at the time only on the plea of necessity. The agents in its execution disliked the task ; and the enemies of the English administration then in power declared it unnecessary. But it attracted but little attention : it did not excite the indignation of the world until some sixteen years had passed. It was not till 1772 that the Abbé Raynal, in his history of the Indies, told the story of a simple peaceful folk living an idyllic and harmless life and brutally torn from their homes, in a way which impressed it on men's minds, and gave it the shape which it has retained, until the documentary discoveries of our own day have given it a somewhat different appearance. In one of Mr. Justin Winsor's invaluable bibliographical notes to his History of America,[*] you will find an instructive history of opinion on the transaction. Mr. Winsor seems to me to be unnecessarily severe towards the Acadians, in a not unnatural reaction from Longfellow's poetical version of their story. But surely we do not need to believe they were models of every virtue before we sympathise with their fate. Theirs was a hard lot, between the upper and the nether millstone: and while we recognise that in that age all governments in the position of the English in Nova Scotia would have felt themselves justified in doing what the English government did, we can rejoice at the increased tenderness of the conscience of the world, which has rendered such a chain of events as led up to the removal of the Acadians impossible for the future. And one word more, before leaving the subject : many of the Acadians managed to return, and their descendents form no incon-

[*] V. 457, *seq.*

siderable element in the population of Nova Scotia and New Brunswick. We cannot but rejoice to find that history is gradually revealing a position of affairs in Nova Scotia during the years 1713-1755, which forbids us to take either the French or the English view of the grievous event. For so long as men feel themselves obliged to take up one or other of these two opposed positions, so long will an obstacle remain in the way of perfect sympathy between the Acadians to-day and their English fellow citizens.

LECTURE VI.

On the Beginnings of Representative Government in Nova Scotia.

We must now turn back and look at the form of government which the English government had set up in the peninsula. In 1714, a Governor had been appointed, with a commission conferring upon him, as was usual in such cases, the functions of commander-in-chief of the forces in the island; those forces, however, being no more than a small garrison in Annapolis. In 1719, the Governor was instructed to "choose a Council for the management of the civil affairs of the Province, from the principal English inhabitants, and, until an Assembly could be formed, to regulate himself by the instructions of the Governor of Virginia."* It is clear that from the first it was intended to create a representative Assembly, as soon as the English population was large enough to make it practicable. In 1720, a Council was nominated consisting of twelve members, and, owing to the paucity of English inhabitants, all save one of these were military or civil officers. From this time onward all important business was brought before the Council at Annapolis, the Governor, or, in his absence, the Lieutenant-Governor, or, in his absence, the Senior Councillor, presiding: and no important decision was taken, except with their approval. In the volume of *Nova Scotia Archives*, already referred to, will be found a series of minutes of Council, with the names of those present, an account of the business laid before them by the Governor, or his deputy, and the orders agreed to,—the latter being usually prefaced with some such words as "Advised and

* Haliburton, 93.

ordered," "Advised and **agreed**," or, "Resolved."* These orders were, however, all of an administrative character, and had to do chiefly with the steps taken to secure an oath of allegiance from the Acadians, and to keep the missionaries under control. The Council also exercised judicial functions, and heard such appeals from the native deputies as the people cared to bring.†

The English population did not increase beyond the handful of officials, the small garrison, and **temporary** detachments of New England troops, and accordingly the system of government remained unaltered until 1749. But **in** that year the English government determined both to strengthen **its** power in Nova Scotia, and to provide for **some** of the soldiers and **mariners** disbanded **after the** peace of **1748, by** the establishment, at **its own expense,** of a colony. Accordingly, an advertisement **was** published in the London **Gazette promising grants of land, in** proportion to their **rank and families, to such of the officers** and private men **lately dismissed His Majesty's land and** sea service as were **willing to settle in Nova Scotia;** and the same conditions **were offered to** "carpenters, shipwrights, smiths, masons, joiners, brickmakers, bricklayers, and all other artificers necessary in building or husbandry." They were promised that as soon as possible "a civil government shall be established, whereby they shall enjoy all the liberties, privileges, **and** immunities enjoyed by His Majesty's subjects in any **other of the** colonies and plantations in America." What, however, **was** far more important, **it was** announced that they shall "be subsisted **during the** passage, also for the space of twelve months after their arrival. They shall be furnished with arms and ammuni-

* e.g. 20, 21, 24, 25, 78.

† *Haliburton* 92, where, in 1731, the Governor complains that "the gentlemen of the Council are daily employed and harassed with their affairs (there being no other Court of Judicature)." It was probably after **this** that the Acadians began to withdraw their suits from the operation **of English law.**

tion, as far as will be judged necessary for their defence, with a proper quantity of materials and utensils for husbandry, clearing and cultivating the lands, erecting habitations, carrying on the fishery, and such other purposes as shall be deemed necessary for their support."* To meet the expenses of this undertaking Parliament voted £40,000.†

Now, I want you to notice that such a plan of emigration organised and directed by government, was for England "a bold and *novel* expedient," to use the language of Mr. Lecky, in describing the measure.‡ It was, however, only doing what the French government had done three quarters of a century before; and it is to the fact that three quarters of a century had elapsed that we must mainly attribute the different social basis on which it was established. The measure illustrates what I have already said as to the insufficiency of ordinary economic motives to bring out independent colonists: nothing save religious zeal, as in the case of New England, was sufficient. The New England colonies are exceptional; in the case of the rest of the European colonies in the New World, until the present century, there were but two ways in which tillers of the soil could be brought over; either by "undertakers" and companies, who bore the expense of their emigration in order to profit by their labours, as in Virginia and New Holland; or by the government.

Some 3760 adventurers with their families accepted the offer; and these under the command of Colonel Cornwallis, the new Governor of Nova Scotia, crossed the ocean, protected by a large military force, and founded the town of Halifax, named after the President of the Board of Trade, to whom its existence was largely due. Cornwallis's commission, which you will find in the *Nova Scotia*

* See the advertisment in *Nova Scotia Archives*, 495.
† Haliburton, i., 38.
‡ *History of England*, i., 480.

Archives, gave him power to nominate a Council, and such other officers as he might judge necessary. With the advice and consent of the said Council he was given authority to summon General Assemblies of the freeholders and planters according to the usage of the rest of our colonies and plantations in America. The **Governor** with the advice and consent of the Council and Assembly was given power to make laws, statutes, and ordinances " which are not to be repugnant but as near as may **be agreeable** to the laws and statutes of this Kingdom of Great Britain. Provided that all such laws, etc., be within three months . . after the making thereof, transmitted to us . . for our disallowance or approbation thereof. And in case any of **the said laws** . . not before confirmed by us, shall at any time be **disallowed and** not approved and so signified by **us** . . unto you or to the Commander in Chief of our said province for the time being, then such and so many of the said laws . . as shall be so disallowed and **not approved, shall from** thenceforth cease, determine, and **become utterly void."** The royal veto in England has fallen into disuse, though it cannot be said that it ceased to be a possibility until after 1832; for though the progress of events had brought it about, long before that time, that no ministry could carry on the business of administration without a majority in the House of Commons, the **exercise** of royal patronage and borough influence made it possible **for** the King to *create* a subservient majority. But the Governor's veto was meant **to be a reali**ty in Nova Scotia. "**To the end that nothing** may **be passed or done by our said Council or Assem**bly to the prejudice **of us, our heirs and successors,** we will and ordain that you, the said Edward Cornwallis, shall have and enjoy a *Negative Voice* in the making and passing of all laws, statutes, and ordinances." He was, of course, **given** power to adjourn, prorogue, and dissolve all General

9

Assemblies. With the advice and consent of the Council he was authorized to establish courts of justice ; and he was entrusted with full military authority.

This commission deserves more attention from Canadian constitutional historians than it has yet received ; for it is the first appearance of the imperial power of disallowance in what is now the Dominion of Canada. It was, however, but the usual form of a Governor's commission at this period; and the clauses quoted above will be found in identically the same language in the commission to the Governor of New York in 1754, and in that to General Murray as Governor of Canada in 1763.*

Cornwallis arrived at Chebucto, determined to bring the new Council into existence with all its executive authority, before permitting his subjects to land. Paul Mascarene, who, as senior councillor for many years at Annapolis, and as Lieutenant-Governor since 1740 in the absence of the Governor in England, had borne almost the whole burden of administering the country, had crossed the peninsula with one of the members of his Council, to meet the new Governor, and these together with one or two officers who had served in the colony, and two or three newcomers from England were sworn in as members of the Council on board Cornwallis's ship.† The province was still to be ruled by a Governor and Council, with much the same powers as before ; but the seat of government was changed ; new blood was brought into the administration ; and the subjects to be ruled were no longer exclusively aliens in religion and language. Then the work of settlement began ; and before the winter set in, Halifax was a town of five thousand inhabitants. Next year the English government made the same announcement in various parts of Germany as they had in England, inviting persons to remove to

---

* Both are given in **Maseres,** *Collection.*

† See thé account by Dr. Akins of *The First Council* in *Collections of the Nova Scotia Historical Society,* vol. ii.

Nova Scotia in ships provided for them by the government, and promising to furnish them with all necessaries and with food for a year after their arrival. An agent at Rotterdam "undertook to transport a thousand foreign Protestants upon the condition of the English government paying him a guinea for each person";* and some 1600 persons, German and Swiss, were brought over at various times during 1751, 1752, and 1753. In 1753, Lunenberg was founded with these foreign settlers; but the hardships of their situation, especially the attacks of the Indians (instigated as it is now proved, by the French government, though it was nominally a time of peace), led to a revolt which was only overpowered by a body of troops from Halifax. Next year the government sent supplies of cattle; and the paternal character of the whole undertaking is amusingly illustrated by the way in which these cattle were distributed, begining with "every two families with good character" receiving one cow and one sheep; or six sheep, one sow, and six goats between them, down to "every two single men of bad character," who received three sheep and one sow between them.†

With so heterogeneous and troublesome a body of settlers, the Governors were not over eager to carry out that portion of their commission which related to the creation of an Assembly. It seems to have been the clerk of the Board of Trade who first called attention to the question whether the Council by itself had any legislative authority, and had any legal power to issue the laws already published by them for the good government of Halifax, and the regulation of its commerce. The Lords Commissioners for Trade and Plantations had the case before the law officers of the Crown,—the Attorney General being then

---

* *Archives*, p. 616; for the rascality of this agent, the overcrowding of the ships, and the decrepit old men despatched for the sake of the guineas, see *Ibid.* 676.

† Haliburton, ii., 131-134.

William Murray, next year to become Lord Chief Justice, as Lord Mansfield,—who returned it as their opinion that "the Governor and Council alone are not authorized by His Majesty to make laws till there can be an Assembly."* In spite of the remonstrances of Governor Lawrence that it was "impossible in our present circumstances to call an Assembly, and that numberless inconveniences would attend the collecting a set of people such as are to be found in this province in that shape," the Board of Trade was inexorable, and ordered the Governor to consult with the Chief Justice of the colony, as to how it could most properly be convened. This was in 1755. The Governor still delayed ; a sufficient excuse was the necessity of proceeding against Louisburg. But when he returned victorious in 1758, the unwelcome task could no longer be deferred. The Council drew up a number of resolutions as to the plan of election—" for the province at large, until the same shall be divided into counties, sixteen members, and for the township of Lunenburg two, and for the township of Halifax two."† These resolutions were transmitted to England, and approved by His Majesty, and the first assembly of Nova Scotia met on the second of October, 1758.

The Assembly immediately justified the expectations of the Governor by quarrelling with the Council and himself. Into the disputes which arose I do not propose to enter ; before we could be in a position to have any opinion worth having, it would be necessary to know not only that it was an elected assembly in opposition to a nominated council, but also what was the character of the community, and of the men who formed the first Assembly, and what were the difficulties in the work of administration.

* *Archives*, 709-711.

† Haliburton, i., 209. By next year the country had been divided into counties, and at the new election two members were returned from each of five counties, four from Halifax and two from three other towns.

There is, however, one matter of more general interest which cannot be passed over, and with some reference to which our narrative of Nova Scotian history may for the present end. In the first session, Haliburton tells us * "the House passed a bill, disqualifying any person filling a situation of profit or emolument under government from holding a seat at the Council board, or being returned as a member of the Assembly; but this bill, as it was considered a direct attack upon them, was rejected by the Council.' Doubtless, the immediate occasion of the measure, and of its rejection, was personal antagonism. But more than this was involved. A clause like this, excluding placeholders from the House of Commons, had been inserted in the English Act of Settlement in 1702, to come into force on the accession of the House of Hanover. Parliament repented before it was too late, and repealed this clause in 1708. Had it not been repealed, that separation between the Executive and Legislative would have been effected in England which is now one of the most important characteristics of the American system. And had this bill of the Nova Scotian Assembly been accepted, the same result would have followed. It is a noteworthy fact that on the occasion of the first session of the first Legislative Assembly of Nova Scotia, a decision should have been arrived at, to which is largely due the practice of Cabinet government that now distinguishes the Canadian from the American constitutional system.

i., 217.

LECTURE VII.

On the Struggle between England and France, and the Conquest of Canada.

WE have now arrived at the period of the English Conquest of Canada. Before, however, we follow the fate of Canada under English rule, let us glance at the general course of events during the preceding half century. The eighteenth century may be characterised in many ways: it was the century in which those forces came to a head which in France destroyed an absolute system of government and a feudal organisation of society; in European politics, it saw the rise of two great military monarchies, the kingdom of Prussia, and the empire of Russia. But if one had to select the one group of events by which the age could be best described, the events to which the eighteenth century will probably in later ages owe its distinction, it would be this:— The eighteenth century witnessed the struggle between England and France for commercial and colonial empire; the victory of England; its consequent loss of such colonial empire as it had hitherto created; and the gain by it, nevertheless, of a second empire, which has not as yet been formally dismembered. The events were perhaps first given their due significance by a remarkable book, Prof. Seeley's *Expansion of England*, which is also of interest for the stimulus it gave to the Imperial Federation movement.

We meet on the threshold a widely diffused popular opinion, which must be removed from the path. It is vaguely supposed that England has always, ever since the early middle ages, occupied something like the position of naval superiority which she has held during this century;

that she has always been mistress of the seas. The truth, however, is, that the accident of **Henry II.**'s marriage with the heiress of Guienne gave the English King during the middle ages, especially during the Hundred Years' War with France, a position in Europe out of all proportion to the resources of England taken by itself; **and that from the time that great national monarchies began to consolidate themselves on the continent, that is, from about the middle of the fifteenth century, England became a second-rate power, and remained so until the eighteenth century. It is not,** I think, possible to doubt this when we notice the attitude of Henry VIII. towards the two great rivals for European supremacy, France and Spain; and the attitude of James I. towards Austria, Spain, France, and Sweden. England's naval power began with the creation of **a fleet under the Commonwealth, and its successful encounters, under Admiral Blake, with the Dutch.** Nor is it accurate **to suppose that English enterprise was always in the van in the work of settlement and discovery. It was preceded by Spain, by Portugal, by Holland, and by France.** Portugal had been united to Spain in 1580, and did not succeed in regaining its independence again till 1640. During that interval, Holland had taken the opportunity to conquer most of the old Portuguese possessions in the East Indies; and when Portugal had regained its freedom it had **lost the** vigour and energy which would have enabled it to struggle with its more powerful rivals. It retained Brazil in **peace, but** fell out of the lists **as a competitor for further possessions. Spain** was crippled by the long **strain upon her resources involved in** the effort of Philip II. **to act as the champion of** Catholicism in Europe, and in the disastrous attempt to subdue the rebellious provinces in the Netherlands. She, also, contented herself in future with the possession of Central America and Peru, **and** fell out of the race. By the beginning of the seven**teenth century, Holland had come** to be the **first commercial** power in Europe. She almost monopolised the carrying trade of Europe: her East India Company rapidly created an eastern empire for her; and she was planting her foot in North America. The position for a century held by the little Republic of the United Netherlands is one of the most remarkable phenomena in European history. A recent historian of English industry and commerce entitles one of his chapters, "Conscious Imitation of the Dutch." They were the models imitated by other states in methods of taxation, in agriculture, in banking. As I have already said, it was the commercial and maritime supremacy of the Dutch which explains the English and French attacks upon them during the period of Cromwell and Charles II. But before the end of the seventeenth century the energies of Holland also were flagging. Her wealth was *mercantile* wealth, not wealth derived from the internal resources of the country. Accordingly the New Netherlands were conquered by the English; the colonial trade of Holland was restricted to the spice islands; and for the defence even of its territory in Europe it was obliged to cling to the English alliance. It seemed likely that her place would be taken by France. France, under Colbert, had leapt to a foremost place among the commercial powers of Europe. Colbert had reorganised the finances; had created new manufactures; had brought all the trading adventures of the country beneath Royal control, and had given them a powerful stimulus; and, in especial, we have seen how in Canada, beginning in 1663, he had established a strong administration and created a settled agricultural population. France, instead of Holland, became the model of European statesmen: and the name of her great minister furnished a designation for the policy henceforth pursued by them all.

Let me briefly explain what "Colbertism" was. Colbert, of course, wished to increase the prosperity, the wealth of France: to this end he wished to remove burdens from agriculture: to create manufacturing industries: to establish colonies which should not only be flourishing themselves, but also enrich the **mother country by trade**. So far there was nothing peculiar in Colbert's action, save the keenness of his insight into the fact that the power of France rested upon her material well being. What, however, was striking, was the amount of importance **he** attached to one particular test of prosperity, and **the influence** of this test upon his policy. Money, it was thought, was—not the *only* wealth, it is an absurd misrepresentation **of** the mercantilists to attribute such a belief to them— but so much more important a form than any other that national prosperity must be estimated by its abundance in a country. The way to increase the **wealth of the country**, therefore, was for a nation to export more than it imported, since the balance must be paid in **gold**. In consequence, the policy **of the** government was **to favour** exports and discourage imports. Exports were to **be favoured by** subsidising manufactures and **giving bounties**; imports, **of** such articles **as could be made in the country, to be** discouraged, by imposing heavy duties. It is easy to see how the colonies from this point of view must have been regarded. They were not supposed to be independent communities, established or permitted to establish themselves, and then left free to pursue their own interest in **their own** way: they were rather regarded as subservient to **the** interest of the mother country, thus **defined**. They were markets in which **the** goods **of the mother country could be sold**: they were the source **whence the mother country could** derive commodities, or **the raw materials of** commodities, which her merchants **could** sell to the **rest** of the world. All European countries treated their colonies in this way—England being distinguished from them only by her comparatively greater liberality. But it was Colbert who first set an impressive example of such a policy.

The struggle between England and France for colonial and mercantile supremacy,—you see now how these two were bound up together,—may be said to have begun with the wars of William III. and Louis XIV., and to have ended with Waterloo. Throughout, this was what was at issue, and throughout it was one of the principal motives in the minds of statesmen. But in the first two wars of that period the question primarily at stake, and the one which engaged most attention, was the maintenance of the balance of Europe against Louis XIV.; and in the last two wars, the main question was the struggle against Revolution and Napoleonic Empire. In the three wars which occupy the central part of that period,—that commonly called the *War of the Austrian Succession*, ending with the of Peace of Aix la Chapelle in 1748, that called the *The Seven Years' War*, ending with the Peace of Paris in 1763, and the *War with France* arising out of the assistance rendered by it to the United States, and ending with the treaty of Versailles in 1783, motives of colonial and mercantile aggrandisement were at least as powerful as motives of European balance. The War of the Austrian Succession was the **preliminary wrestle**: the Seven Years' War was the decisive struggle : **and the third** war was the vain endeavour of France to regain what she had lost. Two things moreover have to be remembered,—that though there was nominally peace between England and France between 1745 and 1756, this peace was observed neither in America nor in India, and the war was practically continuous ; and that it was in time of nominal peace that some of the most important contests took place, especially " the war of the French and Indians," as it was called in New England and the death of Braddock.

The position in America before the Seven Years' War was briefly this : France held Canada and Louisiana—an indefined district on the lower waters of the Mississippi. The problem was, would the English colonies succeed in pushing westward and breaking their communication ; or would the French succeed in establishing a line of forts down the Mississippi and Ohio, connecting Louisiana and Canada, and confining the British colonies to the seaboard, a condition which might not improbably lead finally to their conquest. What the Peace of Paris did was this : alike in India and in America it secured to England the *possibilities* of the future. In India, the French East India Company was obliged to promise not to maintain an armed force ; which meant, not that England had handed over to it at once a great empire, but that henceforth it alone could profit by the opportunities of creating an empire which the condition of India presented. In America, France gave up Canada, and ceded Louisiania to Spain, so that the sole rival of the English was henceforth a weak and unenergetic people. But the almost immediate and not altogether unforeseen result of the peace, was that the English colonies, being relieved by England from the constant dread of the French power in Canada, could venture to declare themselves independent.

The political history of the last few years tends to make us regard the constitutional struggles of the seventeenth and eighteenth centuries, in a light somewhat different from that in which they were viewed twenty or thirty years ago. Events have very largely modified our political ideals, and this especially in two directions. In the first place we are beginning to lose that complete confidence in parliamentary government which was so marked a characteristic of the older Liberalism of Europe and America. Reformers in all countries used to believe that government must inevitably fall ultimately beneath the control of a representative assembly, and that in such assemblies all classes ought to be directly represented ; so that any attempt to delay the creation of representative bodies, any struggle to prevent their obtaining complete legislative and taxative authority and a controlling influence over the composition of the executive, any hesitation in extending the franchise, was regarded as a useless antagonism to righteous forces which must ultimately prevail. Now I will not say that in the minds of thoughtful men such feelings as these have altogether disappeared. It is still believed that the people have a right to determine by what laws they should be governed, in what way their money should be spent, and there seems no method of securing this, save by a representative assembly. But the fresh enthusiasm in favour of government by an elected assembly, which is so naive and touching in the reformers of the earlier years of this century, seems to be passing away. And this for many other reasons, good and bad. All one need here say is, that representative government has been by no means so successful as was anticipated. In France there is a widespread disgust with the Chamber of Deputies which is just now taking the form of Boulangism; in America the House of Representatives has resigned much of its legislative power to small committees, and in the various States there is so keen a distrust of their legislators that in thirty-two out of the thirty-eight States existing in 1888 the sittings of the legislative bodies have been restricted by recent constitutions to once in two years, and in two-thirds of these to a specified number of days in each session. Now this does not throw us back into the arms of absolutism or aristocracy, but it does do this—it saves us from an intellectual idolatry. It makes us see that though in particular circumstances the grant of representative government may have been wise and even necessary, the question of justice at any particular time is not solved merely by the fact that one party desired and the other opposed parliamentary institutions.

The second influence is that created by the movement of *nationality*. There was a time when the movement of nationality, and the struggle for representative institutions seemed to go together. This was especially the case in

Italy and Germany. But what we have been learning during the last twenty years is, that the movement of nationality does **not stop with** the great national groups: it shews itself with equal strength in smaller peoples,— among the Flemings of Belgium, the Czechs of Bohemia, the Croats and Roumanians attached to the kingdom of Hungary. This again adds to the difficulties of representative government. The small nationality, as in the case of Croatia, cannot be denied the right to an Assembly of its own; but if the **unity** of the composite State of **which** it forms part, Hungary, is to be maintained, the central Parliament with a Magyar majority must have a certain authority over the local Assembly; and with existing national antagonisms it is very hard **to get** the Magyar majority **always to act wisely,** or the Croat Assembly to submit.* And another point comes to light : ever since the failure of the untimely measures of Joseph II., it has been evident that **peoples influenced by the spirit of nationality will prefer to retain what, from the point of view of** modern Liberalism, **are obsolete and mediæval institutions,** associated **with their national existence, rather than the** most symmetrical, and, as it might seem, enlightened measures imposed upon them by an alien authority.†

From 1760 to 1763, Canada was under military government. Modern French Canadian writers, such as Garneau, speak of it as "the reign of the soldiery," and attack the English Government **for having** "upset their whole social organisation **to make room for the** most insupportable of **all tyranny, that of courts martial."** But they do not seem **to have much fairly to grumble at.** What they might justly lament **is, that in consequence of the victory** of an English over a French army, their country should **have been** handed over, without the consent of its people, to a foreign ruler. But such conquests and acquisitions of unwilling sub-

---

* See Leger, *History of Austro-Hungary*, 586 seq.
† *Ibid*, ch. 23.

jects were made by all the great powers of the time; and France would, of course, have done the same thing with the English colonies if it could. Indeed, so late as 1871, we have seen the same thing take place in the case of the German annexation of Alsace. Granting the English rule as inevitable, it can hardly be wondered at that, until the war was over, until by the Treaty of Paris the French Government had formally ceded the Province, the English Government should have scarcely thought it worth while to establish a regular government. But at the earliest moment possible, in 1763, an orderly government was established, and a commission issued to a Governor by royal letters patent, of the same character as was usual in other English colonies. There was to be a Governor with a nominated Council, who were to take the usual oaths of allegiance, and subscribe the declaration against transubstantiation; but "so soon as the state and circumstances of the said colonies will admit thereof," a General Assembly with legislative authority was to be summoned. But it was taken for granted that the members of this Assembly would be subject to the same tests as the members of the English House of Commons, and in particular would subscribe the declaration against transubstantiation. The Assembly was therefore to be an exclusively Protestant one, and it was assumed also that the laws to be administered by the tribunals the Governor was empowered to establish were to be the English laws.

LECTURE VIII.

On the Policy of the Quebec Act.

The Quebec Act of 1774 did three things : it created a Legislative Council to be nominated by the Crown: it recognised the Roman Catholic Church, and sanctioned the continuance of the old Canadian ecclesiastical system, including tithes ; and it enacted that the old Canadian law should continue to be in force in civil cases, while in criminal matters the English law was to rule. This latter enactment involved the retention of the seigneurial system: and the maintenance of the old law has, of course, though the use of the French language in the courts is not expressly referred to in this statute, been one of the causes of the subsequent strength of that tongue in the province of Quebec. Accordingly, the Quebec Act demands from us more attention than any subsequent measure.

Let us take each of these three points in turn; and first, as to the Council.

The *twelfth clause* of the Act ran :

"Whereas it may be necessary to ordain many regulations for the future welfare and good government of the province of Quebec, etc., and whereas it is at present inexpedient to call an Assembly, it shall . . be lawful for His Majesty, etc., by warrant under his signet and sign manual, and with the advice of the Privy Council, to constitute and appoint a Council for the affairs of the Province of Quebec to consist of . . persons resident there, not exceeding twenty-three nor less than seventeen . . which Council . . or the major part thereof shall have power and authority to make ordinances for the peace, welfare, and good government of the said province, with the consent of His Majesty's Governor, or in his absence, of the Lieutenant-Governor, or Commander in Chief for the time being."

Clause XIII. "Provided always, that nothing in this Act contained shall extend to authorize or impower the said Legislative Council to lay any taxes or duties within the said Province, such rates and taxes only excepted as the inhabitants of any town or district may be authorized by the said Council to assess, levy, and apply, within the said town or district, for the purpose of making roads, erecting or repairing public buildings, or for any other purpose respecting the local convenience and economy of such town or district."

Clause XIV. Provided also, . . . that every ordinance so to be made shall, within six months, be transmitted by the Governor, . . and laid before His Majesty for his Royal approbation ; and if His Majesty shall think fit to disallow thereof, the same shall cease and be void from the time that His Majesty's Order in Council thereupon shall be promulgated in Quebec."

The Governor had already the assistance of a Council for executive purposes: but it was held, as it had been held in Nova Scotia, that under the terms of his commission, the Council had no legislative authority legislation was reserved for the consent, in addition to the Council, of a Representative Assembly, "so soon as the state and circumstances of the Colony permitted." Legislative authority was now conferred upon a nominated Council, and it is declared inexpedient to call an Assembly. That this contention was true can hardly be doubted. Contemporary estimates of the population in Canada widely differ; but it is probable that the French numbered at least 75,000 or 80,000, the English at most 500 or 600. It would, under these circumstances, have been absurd to have imposed English parliamentary test oaths, and so created an exclusively Protestant Assembly. Could not Catholics have been permitted to vote and to sit in the Assembly? In that case it would have been almost exclusively Catholic. The Protestant feeling of England at this time was so strong that it would have been dangerous for either party definitely to make such a proposal. But even if this danger were not to be feared, there were two objections: in the first place, Lord North believed that to put so much power into the hands of an elective French Assembly, at a time when it was very likely that France would make another great effort to recover her lost possessions, would be extremely imprudent; in the second place, there is not the least evidence that the French Canadians desired an Assembly,—indeed, it is pretty clear that they took no interest in the matter. If they thought of it at all, it was only to fear that if they had an Assembly they would have to pay the expenses of government.* It is very instructive to notice the way the matter was avoided by the opposition leaders in the discussions on the Quebec Bill in the House of Commons. You will remember that Lord North was then in power, with a Tory majority and the support of the King; that among the leaders of the Whig opposition were Fox and Burke; that the Ministry was in the midst of its struggle with the American Colonies, and engaged in its contest with Wilkes and the Whig corporation of London. During the duration of the Parliament from 1768 to 1774, the order for the exclusion of strangers was so rigidly enforced that no reports of the debates appeared, and the Parliament was known as "The Unreported Parliament." But very complete short-hand notes were taken by one of the members, Sir Henry Cavendish, and in 1841 these notes were published under the name of the Cavendish Debates. The printing of the reports, how-

* Cf. Cavendish, *Debates on the Canada Bill*, 162. They had alleged this very reason in a petition to the King in 1773, signed by a number of Canadian seigneurs and merchants, urging that a Council partly composed of Canadians would be far more suitable for the time being.

ever was suspended with the year 1771 : but, fortunately, the interest aroused by the Union Bill had induced the editor, in 1839, to publish the debate on the Quebec Act in a separate volume. From this we are able to follow every turn in the discussion, and all the devices and humours of party warfare.

The Whigs were ready enough to take up any constitutional cry, but this matter of an assembly perplexed them. Their supporters in the country generally, if not their parliamentary leaders, were attacking other parts of the bill because it established Popery, so that they could not well demand the formation of a Popish Assembly. At the same time they could not decently ask for a Protestant Assembly representing not one in a hundred and fifty of the population—especially as some of their better men were at this very time advocating the removal of Catholic disabilities in England and Ireland. All the opposition could do therefore was to declaim vaguely against the "establishment of a despotic government, contrary to the genius and spirit of the British Constitution." When it came to the discussion of these particular clauses, Fox touched upon them as lightly as possible, and carefully guarded himself at the outset against any attempt to fix upon him the responsibility of demanding an assembly. "That I can contradict this assertion and say it is expedient to call an assembly, I will not assert ; but from all the information I have obtained in this house, I am inclined to think it is expedient."*

Secondly, as to the *Church*. The clauses on this head met with hardly more real opposition than those relating to the Council. They run as follows :

Clause V. "For the more perfect security and ease of the minds of the inhabitants of the said province, it is hereby declared that His Majesty's subjects professing the religion of the Church of Rome . . may have, hold, and enjoy the free exercise of the religion of the Church

* Cavendish, *Debates*, p. 246.

of Rome, . . and that the clergy of the said Church may hold, receive, and enjoy their accustomed dues and rights, with respect to such persons only as shall profess the said religion."

Clause VI. "Provided, nevertheless, that it shall be lawful for His Majesty, his heirs, etc., to make such provisions out of the rest of the said accustomed dues and rights (*i. e.* tithes or lands which had passed into the hands of Protestants), for the encouragement of the Protestant religion, and for the maintenance and support of a Protestant clergy within the said province as he shall from time to time think necessary and expedient."

The object of the government was to retain the provincial endowment of religion, but to cause it to be employed for the maintenance of whatever church or churches the people themselves chose. For the present, all the tithes from Catholics were to go to Catholic priests,—there were so few Protestant holders of land that it was not necessary to take any very immediate action with regard to their tithes,—but by and by, if their numbers should increase, their tithes were to go in like manner to Protestant clergy. It was precisely the same principle as that which allows the education taxes of Protestants in Quebec to go to Protestant schools, and of Catholics in Ontario to Catholic schools. There is, indeed, an obvious difference in that everybody now believes in the endowment of education, and that most persons in the English speaking provinces of Canada do not now believe in the endowment of religion. But in justice to the ministry of Lord North, it must be remembered that at that time, only a small part of the English people—the Independents—objected on principle to a state endowment of religion. The same was true in America. In all the American colonies I believe, except Pennsylvania, there was a state endowment of religion. This was abolished at the Revolution in the Southern States, where Episcopacy had been established, but chiefly because the Episcopalian clergy had taken the English side. But in New England, the endowment of Congregationalism did not come to an end in Massachusetts till 1811, nor in Connecticut till 1818. When the American colonies protested against the Quebec Act, it was not against the endowment of religion, but against the endowment of the Roman Catholic religion.

I am not sufficiently acquainted with the history of Quebec to be able to say whether any attempt was made to employ the tithes of Protestants in the way indicated. Let me, however, confirm what I have said as to the policy of the minority by a quotation from one of the Solicitor-General's speeches: "I agree that the Roman Catholic religion ought to be the established religion of that country, in its present state; the clergymen of which are paid by the landed revenue of that country. I do not mean to assert that this should be perpetually the state of Canada; or that we are by law to enact that the people are not to be converted; or that the tithe shall remain to the Popish clergy, or that the tithe shall sink. I would not not hold out the temptation, that if you are a convert you shall not pay tithe. . . Popish clergy should be maintained by such as are Papists; but the money of the Protestants ought to be applied for the maintenance of Protestant clergy. In proportion as the scale with regard to numbers shall turn to the Protestant side, the clergymen ought to be Protestant. Though I wish to tolerate the Popish religion, I do not wish to encourage it. When we tell the Roman Catholics of Canada that we will not oppress them, we at the same time tell the followers of the Church of England that whenever their faith shall prevail, it will have a right to its establishment."*

When the discussion in the Commons reached this clause, there was very little direct fighting against the mainten-

* *Debates*, 218-219.

ance of the existing endowment; some of the opposition urged that the Bishop might prove himself dangerous, but the only point insisted on by the leader of the opposition was as to the propriety of giving the King a discretion in the matter of the tithes of Protestants,—Burke going so far as to propose they should be paid to the Society for the Propagation of the Gospel. How far Burke was from being opposed to the payment of tithes by Catholics for the maintenance of Catholic priests, is seen from his speech: "You have got a people professing the Roman Catholic religion, and in possession of a maintenance legally appropriated to its clergy. Will you deprive them of that? Now that is not a question of 'establishment:' the establishment was not made by you, it existed before the treaty; no Legislature has a right to take it away; no Governor has a right to suspend it. This principle is confirmed by the usage of every civilised nation of Europe. In all our conquered colonies, the established religion was confirmed to them. [You will remember the instance I have already given of Nova Scotia in 1713.] . . What I desire is, that every one should contribute towards the maintenance of the religion he professes; and if this is proper to be done, why not do it immediately? . . I maintain that everyone ought to contribute to the support of some religion or other. Does any gentleman choose to say that the impious profligate, the moment he chooses to avow himself an unbeliever, can appropriate to his own use the tithe he has been accustomed to pay for the support of any religious establishment? Suppose one of those persons should turn Jew: I would give him complete toleration, but I say, let him support the synagogue. I will suppose this case: when a man is sued for his tithe, he will declare that he does not profess the Roman Catholic religion. He then walks directly into that mass house or church for the support of which he has positively refused to engage himself. Suppose he abstracts himself from all religion, he pays no

tithe. If this be allowed, you are encouraging him to be
an atheist."* This was the attitude of the great Whig
leader. In their resistance to the bill, the Whig chiefs
were no doubt supported by a great body of opinion in
England, created by mere Protestant bigotry; but their
party, as a whole, was too much identified with the cause
of toleration, their leading men, Fox and Burke, were too
sincerely the friends of Catholic emancipation in England
and Ireland, for them to take up the No Popery cry. It
was only a free lance like Col. Barré who could venture to
oppose the bill on the ground that it would be too popular
with French Canadians. "A very extraordinary indul-
gence is given to the inhabitants of this Province, and one
calculated to gain the hearts and affections of these people.
To this I cannot object, if it is to be applied to good purposes; but if you are about to raise a Popish army to
serve in the colonies—from this time, all hope of peace in
America will be destroyed. . . I smelt the business
out from the beginning."† The proposal to recognize
Catholicism, and permit its endowment to continue, had
indeed excited the most vehement remonstrances from the
New England colonies,—though in less than a year Congress itself sent commissioners, including Franklin, into
Canada with power to promise that if they would join the
confederation ecclesiastical matters should be entirely left
to a free Legislature constituted by the Canadians themselves, with this limitation only that the Catholic majority
should not exclude Protestants from filling civil offices or
oblige such to pay tithes.‡

* *Ibid.*, 223-224.
† *Ibid.*, 228.
‡ Garneau, *History of Canada*, trans. Bell, II. 147. These instructions
were dated March 20, 1775. On September 5 of the previous year the
Congress had drawn up an Address to the people of Great Britain, pro-
testing among other matters against the Quebec Act, and declaring "we
cannot suppress our astonishment that a British Parliament should ever
consent to establish in that country a religion that has deluged your

No one, I think, who reads the history of the American invasion in 1775-6, and notices how powerful was the support given by the Catholic clergy to the English rule, can deny that from the point of view of British empire, the policy of the Quebec Act was wise. Nor can any one deny that so far as it related to the French Canadians, the action was just. That a country could be annexed against the will of its inhabitants was a barbarous thing enough. That when once annexed, it should be treated as far as possible as a people who had voluntarily put themselves under a common sovereign with another people while retaining their own institutions, was at any rate, one step out of barbarism. The analogy of Scotland, alike in religion and laws, is here significant. But sometimes people overlook the fact that if the British government had not permitted the maintenance of the tithe system, the Americans would have seized the opportunity to do so, and that there would soon have ceased to be a British Canada at all. It is suggested that it might have been expedient to be unjust—which is of course what is meant under the phrase "using the right of the conqueror." Expedient for whom? For Quebec? That is a matter within the competence of Quebec to decide, and if she thinks it inexpedient she can abolish it. Expedient for England—surely it is obvious that the tie between England and Quebec has been the stronger instead of the weaker in consequence. For the Dominion? Well, that is arguable; but the Dominion had not then come into existence; and the British government of 1774 can hardly be attacked because it could not anticipate a condition of things which did not appear till 1867. We have here as so often in history to recognize this—that a peculiar course of action may afterwards turn

island in blood, and dispersed impiety, bigotry, persecution, murder, and rebellion through every part of the world:" quoted in Christie, *History of Lower Canada*, i. 9.

out to have results which are, or seem to be, evil, and yet at the time that particular course may have been the only **just one,** and even the only possible one.

It was over the third feature of the Act, the retention in part of the old Canadian laws, that the battle most fiercely raged.

Clause IV. " **Whereas the provisions** made by the said Proclamation **(of** 1763), etc., have been found upon **experi**ence to be inapplicable to the state and circumstances of the Province, the inhabitants whereof amounted at the conquest to **above 65,000 persons** professing the religion of the **Church of Rome, and** enjoying an established form of constitution **and system** of laws, by which their persons and property had been protected, governed, and ordered, for a long **series** of years from the first establishment of the said **Province of Canada.** Be it enacted that the said proclamation . . and all and every ordinance and ordinances made by the Governor and Council of Quebec (including therefore those embracing the English law) are hereby revoked," etc.

Clause **VIII.** " **Be it enacted, that** all His Majesty's Canadian **subjects** . . the religious orders and communities alone excepted, may **also** hold and enjoy their property and possessions, together with all customs and **usages relative thereto, and** all other their civil rights **in as large,** ample, and beneficial a manner as if **the** said **proclamation, etc., had** not been made, . . **and** that in all matters of contoversy, relative to property and civil rights, resort shall be had to the laws of Canada as the rule for the decision of the same, and all causes that shall hereafter be instituted in any of the Courts of Justice.

. **shall be** determined agreeable to the said **laws and customs of Canada, until** they shall be **varied or altered by** ordinances passed by the Governor . . with the advice and consent of the Legislative Council."

Clause XI. "Whereas the certainty and lenity of the criminal law of England, and the benefits . . . resulting from the use of it have been sensibly felt by the inhabitants, from an experience of more than nine years, be it enacted that the same shall continue to be administered, and shall be observed as law in the Province of Quebec, as well in the description and quality of the offence as in the mode of prosecution and trial," etc.

It was, in fact, the maintenance of the condition of things which had actually arisen since 1763. There had been little objection to the English criminal law,—indeed it was welcomed as preferable to the old system with the judicial powers with which it entrusted the seigneurs, and it had been enforced without much difficulty; but in civil matters disputants had preferred to settle their quarrels out of Court in accordance with their old laws, or, when cases had been presented, the Judges had paid regard to Canadian precedents. The Governor had, indeed, taken upon himself, with questionable legality, but with a view of meeting the circumstances, to issue an ordinance directing the Judges to admit Canadian laws and customs in civil suits.

In the debates in the English House of Commons, however vigorous might be the attack of the opposition on the introduction of a foreign law which was denounced as opposed to the principles of the British Constitution, the contest turned only on a question of degree. Nobody, it is a pleasure to see, proposed that wholesale introduction of the English real property law to a country still in an earlier stage of development, which had wrought so much evil in Ireland. The representative of the English party in Quebec, Mr. Maseres, expressly proposed "the restoration of their family customs, as tenures of land, the mode of conveying, (the law of) marriage, descent, and dower, and the rule in case of persons dying intestate" (*i. e.*, of division between sons, and not the giving of all to the eldest son, as in England), on the ground "that they would not be happy without it;" and argued that as "the laws of tenure contain the laws that oblige the tenants to pay their quit rent, and corn rent, and mutation fines to their landlord, to grind their corn at his mill and give him his meal toll;' they could not be altered without taking away the property of the seigneur, which cannot be done, because it is granted by the capitulation."*

* Cavendish, *Debates*, 126, 133.

LECTURE IX.

The same Subject, continued.

In the last lecture I had touched on the third of **the three parts** of the Quebec Act—the clause relating to the *legal system henceforth to be employed*. I pointed out that at the time it was being discussed in England and Canada, there was no question of any such sweeping revolution as the introduction of the whole of the English legal system. It was entirely a question of degree—how much of the old French **law** should be allowed to remain ? And it was precisely **that** part of the French law which has most sharply **separated Quebec from the other provinces,—the** law relating **to the tenure of land—that no one proposed** to alter. The **policy of introducing a considerable portion of** English law was **defended by the Attorney-General of the Province, Francis Maseres**; yet in a careful and detailed opinion presented to the King in 1769, be expressly recommended that an ordinance should be passed reviving the French laws of tenure, inheritance, dower, alienation, and encumbrance of landed property, and of the distribution of the effects of persons dying intestate. As to the feudal **laws** of tenure these cannot, he argues, be abolished with**out** breaking the promise made in the capitulation of **1760 to preserve to the Canadians the enjoyment of all their** estates **both noble and ignoble. As to the law relating to** the alienation, **mortgaging, and other** incumbering of landed property, he argues that they were not absolutely necessary to the enjoyment of estates and therefore were not necessarily involved in the promises of the capitulation. But he thought they were so closely connected with the **law of tenure** that many practical difficulties would arise from their abolition ; and he goes on to use an argument which is worthy of the attention of those who attribute a peculiar unreasonableness to the French law.

" He conceives it will be the more necessary to revive or continue the French laws upon the subject in order to prevent the introduction of the English laws upon the same subject, viz., the doctrine of estates-tail, the statute *de donis*, the method of defeating that statute by common recoveries, the doctrine of fines, the statute of uses and the doctrine of uses in general, and other nice doctrines relating to real estates which are full of so much subtlety, intricacy, and variety, that if they were to be introduced into this Province they would throw all the inhabitants of it, without excepting even the English lawyers, into an inextricable maze of confusion."

As to the French law concerning dower, and the inheritance of lands, and the distribution of the goods of intestates, Maseres argued that the King was not bound by the capitulation, to retain it ; and in his opinion it had defects which might make it desirable after a time to modify it. But he did not think it necessary to do this at once, and in order "to preserve the tranquility of the Province, and to give satisfaction to the bulk of Canadians it might be better to postpone those important changes."*

After such an opinion as this, I will only make two remarks: I. The French law, feudal as it was, kept upon the soil a large population of small peasant holders of land. The result of the early destruction of feudalism in England has been the sweeping away of this class, and the creation of difficulties in the condition of the agricultural population which England has not yet overcome. *Grande culture*, the system of large farms, certainly has economic advantages, but it has as clearly political disadvantages, and until we see more clearly than we do at present how to remedy these disadvantages, we may be thankful that

* Maseres, *Collection*, 55.

the Quebec Act has helped to maintain a peasant proprietary in one of the Canadian Provinces. II. It was precisely this part of the old French law, as was indeed natural, that the Canadians were most anxious to retain. "At the apprehension" of a change "they had expressed great uneasiness," said General Carleton, the Governor General, in his evidence before the House of Commons, "and more warmth than is usual for that people: they seemed determined to form associations and compacts to resist the English law, if they should be compelled to do it, so far as they could do so with decency;"* and when he was satirically asked what was the nature of those decent compacts to resist the laws of this country, he replied, " to bind themselves in all marriage contracts that all their possessions should go according to the Canadian customs, and in general, to adhere to them as closely and firmly as possible."†
As I said in the last lecture, when we notice the amount of support the Americans met with in their invasion of Quebec in the following year, it is difficult not to conclude that if the Canadians had been still further alienated by a foolish attempt to abolish their cherished customs, there would now be no Dominion of Canada to argue about.

On the other hand the English criminal law, barbarous as it might be in its penalties, was yet not sufficiently different from French law to excite any opposition, and it was probably an advantage to the peasant to abolish the criminal jurisdiction of the seigneur. During the discussion, therefore, it was assumed as a matter of course that the English criminal law should be introduced, and the ministers were able to argue very fairly that as it was in criminal matters that the jury was of greatest importance for protecting the liberty of the subject, the English merchants and adventurers who had gone to Quebec had, in the main, been granted the protection of English law which they claimed.

* Cavendish, *Debates*, 103.
† *Ibid.* iii.

The only real difference of opinion, therefore, concerned part of the civil law, especially that part which would be of most interest to English merchants in Quebec, viz., the law of contract and the procedure relating to it. Now, I do not think it was alleged that the French law of contract was in itself inferior to the English; indeed, the English Chief Justice of Quebec declared that "the Canadian system of laws was much less complicated than the English, and contained in a much less number of books."

The English party seemed to be anxious only for two things, which were rather matters of procedure than of substantive law. One was, arrest for debt, a method of dealing with debtors which they thought more for their interest than the much milder method of Canadian law. But even Maseres admits in his report that he is inclined to think arrests of the body in the first instance an unnecessary piece of harshness in civil suits.* Doubtless, the Whig orators in the House of Commons were disinclined to make much of this grievance on the part of the English traders, and in the Parliamentary debates it was discreetly veiled behind a vague demand for the protection of English law.

The other and more important demand was, the right to have a jury in civil cases. This was an institution to which the French Canadians were altogether unused, and one repugnant to their habits of thought. They had little confidence in the verdicts of jurors, men like themselves, when compared with the decisions of trained Judges; and here it may be remarked that, no matter how much corruption and peculation there may have been in other parts of the old *régime*, there is abundant evidence in the testimony of the Chief Justice, the Attorney-General, and the Governor of Quebec, that the administration of justice had been just, speedy, and cheap.

* Maseres, *Collection*, 23.

The seigneurs were unwilling to have their suits submitted to juries composed in part of their inferiors; and the lower classes grumbled at the burden of attendance. Indeed, so foreign was the jury to their habits of thought that the Chief Justice declared that very often he could not induce a Canadian jury to give any verdict at all; and he added: " I am ashamed to say I did not punish them for it."* Accordingly, the representatives of the merchants and the Whig leaders, had the common sense not to propose that a jury of the English pattern should be necessary in all civil suits in which it was required in England; but only that either of the parties to an action should have the option of calling for a jury : that the jurymen should be paid a fair sum for their trouble : that there should be fifteen or some other uneven number of them : and that the verdict should go by a bare majority.†

Well, now, it is hardly worth while to consider the pros and cons of such a proposal. By this time we see that the claim for the introduction of English law narrowed itself to a comparatively small matter. Whichever way the Government decided their action would do but little to determine whether Quebec should or should not be a French province.

These practical considerations exempt us from the necessity of considering the abstract question, whether England would have been justified, if she had deemed it wise in transforming the whole body of Canadian law. Certainly, however, she would not have had the enlightened International law, even of her own time, upon her side. The right of the conqueror can only be maintained on the ground on which it was maintained in earlier times,—that because you have a right to slay your enemy, you have a right to impose upon him any conditions up to the point

* Cavendish, *Debates*, 152.

† See especially the speeches of the Attorney-General and Solicitor-General, *Ibid.* 265-6, 275-8.

of death. But no authority would hold that the conqueror had a right to slay non-combatants who had peacefully yielded. Grotius, as Thurlow pointed out, had expressly laid down that when empire over another people was obtained, it was right to leave them their domestic institutions. However, to discuss the subject is to fight about shadows. If England had not granted these terms to the conquered, the United States would have done so. This is proved by their action in regard to Louisiana. Louisiana was bought by the United States from France in 1803. Almost at once a number of Louisianian lawyers were appointed to draw up a code based on the previous French and Roman law there observed, and this was issued to the Courts in 1808. English criminal law was introduced just as in England, but the old civil law they were permitted to retain. In the circular of the American Governor Claiborne occurs the following suggestive passage: "Indispensable as (under existing circumstances) has been the adoption of the digest, it will nevertheless be much censured by many native citizens of the United States who reside in the territory. . . For myself, I am free to declare the pleasure it would give me to see the laws of Orleans assimilated to those of the States generally, not only from a conviction that such laws are for the most part wise and just, but from the opinion I entertain that, in a country where unity of government and interests exists, it is highly desirable to introduce throughout the same laws and customs. We ought to recollect, however, the peculiar circumstances in which Louisiana is placed; nor ought we to be unmindful of the respect due to the sentiments and wishes of the ancient Louisianians, who compose so great a proportion of the population."* Imagine, if it

* Gayarré, *History of Louisiana.* iv. 198. I was not aware when I wrote this that there was an argument in support of this position stronger even than the analogy of Louisiana, viz., that the American Congress actually indicated its willingness to acquiesce in the retention of the

is possible, that England had managed to abolish the old law and yet to keep possession of Canada, and that now impassioned orators were denouncing English tyranny, and pointing to the juster policy of the United States!

On the whole, the system of government established by the Quebec Act worked well, and justified the hopes of its creators. One important addition to the constitutional machinery was made in the seventeen years between 1774 and 1791—the creation by the Governor, in 1776, in accordance with his instructions, of a smaller Executive Council, of five members. It was not for many years, however, that the importance of this step came to be recognised. To the Legislative Council the Governor was practically obliged to appoint English residents of wealth and influence, even if they were opposed to his policy, and more likely than not to put difficulties in his way; and therefore he felt the want of some body of councillors sympathising with his general policy, with whom he could deliberate on the measures to be brought before the Legislative Council. This Executive Council, nominated by the representative of the Sovereign and responsible to him, came later to be composed of a committee of the majority in the Legislature, just as in England the ministry came to be practically a committee of the dominant party in the House of Commons; but such was not its original character. It is necessary to keep this transition in view, and to avoid

French civil law if Canada would join in the rebellion. In their address to the inhabitants of the province of Quebec, dated October 26, 1774, while they explain the virtues of trial by jury and *habeas corpus* as "rights" the Canadians were "entitled to," they also insist on the right of the people to be "ruled by laws which they themselves approve," and insinuate a doubt whether the English government really intended to leave the Canadians their old civil law : "Are the French laws in civil cases restored? It seems so. But observe the cautious kindness of the ministers who pretend to be your benefactors. The words of the statute are, that those laws shall be the rule, until they shall be varied or altered by any ordinances of the Governor and Council?" This address will be found in Christie i., 17.

the use of language—such as we find in Garneau—implying that the early Governors were to blame in nominating only their partisans as members of the Executive Council. Its original object was not to act as an additional check upon the Governor, but to assist him in carrying out his policy.

Successful as the new system of government was upon the whole, for it satisfied the inhabitants of the Province and kept it in the possession of the English King during the American invasion, certain difficulties shewed themselves which were inherent in the situation. Prominent English merchants could hardly be kept out of the Legislative Council, and there they renewed the old dispute as to the introduction of English law. In 1785, the Home Government directed the Legislative Council to issue an ordinance establishing the law of *Habeas Corpus*,—probably only to quiet discontent, for it is almost certain that no difficulty would have arisen in obtaining a writ of *Habeas Corpus* as the law already stood. Unfortunately, a Chief Justice Smith had been appointed, strongly in favour of the introduction of English law, who maintained that the Quebec Act did not deprive Englishmen of the right to have recourse to English law when the action lay between Englishmen only, and that it did not prohibit the introduction of English mercantile law. The result was a very general uncertainty as to the state of law in the Province, and much divergence of practice among the Judges.

As to a Legislative Assembly, for a while the English party as a body acquiesced in the decision of the Quebec Act. As one of their chief representatives said in 1784: "It is doubtful whether there would be any advantage in our having a Legislative Assembly in the present state of the country; for the old subjects of the King, namely, those British born would have no chance of being elected by people of the French Canadian race."

The question was revived in 1783-5, with the settlement of the United Empire Loyalists in Nova Scotia, New Brunswick, the Eastern Townships, and Upper Canada. It is hardly necessary to say that the British Government repaid their unselfish patriotism by the utmost possible liberality—by a compensation for their losses amounting to fifteen million dollars, by conveying them to new homes, and maintaining them during the earlier months of their struggle with nature. Accordingly, from the United Empire Loyalists came the warmest friends of the British Government. Yet they had all been accustomed to representative institutions in the colonies from which they had fled—and it is curious to notice how, but a year after the continental part of Nova Scotia had been colonised, the home government thought it necessary to create a new Province of New Brunswick, and give its inhabitants a Legislative Assembly (1784). With such an example, the demand for similar institutions was sure to go up from Upper Canada; and the English party in the Province of Quebec joined in it, hoping to secure a Representative Assembly for the *whole* of the old Province, including Upper Canada, and by the votes of the new English incomers, to counterbalance the French vote in Lower Canada. Meanwhile, among the French themselves, had grown up a party, not large, but able to make itself heard, which joined them in the demand for an elective Assembly; partly influenced by the liberal ideas of the time, partly because they hoped to find in a French Assembly a security for the French law and the Church which they could not find in the Legislative Council. The government cut the knot with the Constitutional Act —with the express object of giving legislative authority in Lower Canada to a French Assembly, and so overcoming the difficulties in the maintenance of the old law which had been created by the Legislative Council; and of giving like power to an English population in Upper Canada.

Great was the disappointment of the small English minority in Quebec. But many as were the difficulties which presented themselves in the working of the Act of 1791, it is scarcely possible to doubt that an attempt at that time to combine the two races in one Council and Assembly would have led to anarchy.

www.ingramcontent.com/pod-product-compliance
Lightning Source LLC
Chambersburg PA
CBHW020859160426
43192CB00007B/988